TV USA

AN ATLAS FOR CHANNEL SURFERS

TV USA

AN ATLAS FOR CHANNEL SURFERS

ROBB PEARLMAN

UNIVERSE

CONTENTS

INTRODUCTION

"I want to go to there."
—Liz Lemon, head writer and showrunner, *TGS with Tracy Jordan.*

If television has taught us anything—and let's face it, television has taught us *everything*—it's that there's a big world outside. A world much more panoramic than the 60" you've got mounted to your wall. Not a black-and-white world, but one so colorful it requires nearly annual upgrades to see it all in as high a definition as possible. A world far more complex than a simple ABC (or CBS or NBC), and one so varied in both acronyms and content that it can be enjoyed in any number of ways: live, recorded, on demand, streamed, cabled, satellited, or antennaed. So big, so colorful, so wide-ranging that it can be overwhelming enough to keep you firmly planted on your couch surfing the airwaves than heading to the beach to surf actual waves.

Rather than using your television set (or computer monitor, phone, or tablet) as merely a window into other vistas, let its more than seventy-five years of programming serve as your personal travel agent. From pilots to finales to very special episodes and from coast to coast, the United States provides something for everyone. Whether you're looking for a quaint inn in Maine to spend a weekend antiquing, heading to LA with your bongo-playing husband on the lookout for celebrities, recently moved to Atlanta and looking for a new decorator, or searching for a hip piano bar while visiting your Grandma and her roommates in Miami, *TV USA* is the only guidebook you'll ever need.

Even if you're a guest star visiting from out of town, a wacky neighbor, or part of an ensemble, you're sure to find lots of places to vacation or settle into a new slot of your own.

And remember, a powered-down screen does nothing but turn into a mirror that reflects your own disappointments, fears, and demons back at you—in 4K—so keep your television on and boldly go!

FOREWORD BY FRANK DeCARO

In 1994, a group of young newspaper and magazine writers—myself included—attended a journalism conference in Minneapolis, a city which many of us from the East Coast had never visited.

There were two major things on our collective agenda that week: one, promote fair, inclusive, and accurate representation in the media; and, two, visit the carved-up Victorian where Mary Richards and Rhoda Morgenstern rented apartments from Phyllis Lindstrom.

Not necessarily in that order.

There were no smartphones, no GPS apps, in those days, as you may remember, so we had no idea where that subdivided manse actually was. But we did what you did back then when you didn't know where you were going. We piled into a taxi and told the driver, "Take us to the *Mary Tyler Moore* show house!" And, with the meter running and no hesitation at all, he did.

He deposited us in a quiet, affluent neighborhood to which some before us—and many after—have made a pop-culture pilgrimage.

As it turns out, though that TV house is very real, the street address fans of the show, a timeless sitcom about a single woman who could turn the world on with her smile, know as well as they know their own, doesn't actually exist in real life.

But, oh, in our hearts and minds does it ever.

That's the power of television. TV makes the fictional—and the *fictionalized*—so very palpable. Mary Richards, an associate producer of the nightly news at WJM, never *really* served Veal Prince Orloff to (and then took most of it back from) her boss, Lou Grant, in that house. But why quibble over such dinner-party details? She did so in our imaginations, and every once in a while, preferably late at night, she does it again and again. Reruns are a wonderful thing.

So is this book.

TV USA: An Atlas for Channel Surfers does for readers what that Minneapolis cab driver did for us, all those years ago. It takes you to places you think you know, but don't really: like the Miami of *The Golden Girls* from lanai to Rusty Anchor, the Milwaukee of *Happy Days* and *Laverne & Shirley*—where bikers and bottle-cappers ate pizza and bowled, but rarely *vo-de-oh-do-do*'ed—and the Cincinnati of *WKRP in . . .*, where on one particularly *fowl* Thanksgiving, it actually rained turkeys. Oh, the humanity.

On shows like these, not to mention classic dramas like *Grey's Anatomy*, *Twin Peaks*, and *Route 66*, the location became almost a character itself, whether the garlic-rubbed New Jersey of *The Sopranos*, the fashion-mad Manhattan of *Sex and the City*, the crayon-colored Springfield of *The Simpsons*, or the often-rainy City of Brotherly Love in *It's Always Sunny in Philadelphia*.

If only there were an Emmy for Best Supporting Architecture!

The most beloved TV shows in history—there are about 1,200 memorialized in this book—influence how we feel about these burgs long before we ever visit them. They make us want to visit these places, if only to take a selfie with the burnished Henry Winkler statue known as the "Bronze Fonz" on a RiverWalk in Wisconsin, or pose in front of the Great Northern Hotel in Washington State, where the owls *still* are never quite what they seem.

Read this wonderful tome and then use it to plan a trip to your favorite location. Wherever that might be, *TV USA* will help you get there, even if you never deign to put down your remote and actually leave your armchair.

I'll tell you this, though: If you ever do make it to Minneapolis after all, bring a hat. Even on the coldest day, you're going to want to toss it in air.

As
with any journey,
this road trip might turn down
some roads where you might see
some sights you think are in the wrong
places (or places you've seen before). So
before you get car sick, please remember that
this adventure, which may miss some spots
along the way, was mapped out to be as
GPS-accurate as possible, and some
judgment calls had to be made to
make it a satisfying jaunt for
all travelers.

An auspicious start to any alphabetical listing of states, Alabama is the sweet home to about 4.9 million residents, but fewer television shows than appear on even one of Bart Simpson's hands. twenty-second to join the Union, but first in the hearts of millions of college football fans, it offers residents and tourists a wealth of things to do, from Mobile's beautiful beaches to historic sites in Birmingham and Montgomery.

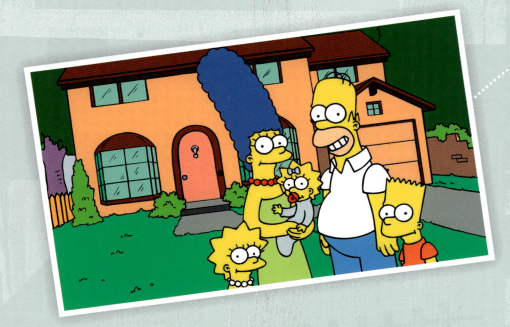

THE SIMPSONS
Springfield 1989–present

If you're looking for places where Springfield locals dine, check out the fine Italian served at Luigis, the warm beer at Moe's, and of course, Lard Lad Donuts, home to the most drool-worthy treats you'll ever have.

HART OF DIXIE
Bluebell (fic.) 2011–2015
Bluebell, Alabama's Rammer
Jammer, owned by former bartender
Wade Kinsella, caters to locals and
tourists alike with a full menu and a
bevy of annual events, including the
Gumbo Cook-Off, the Super Bowl
party, or even a Passover Seder!

TV USA

ALASKA

I can see TV from here! Which is great, because not many shows are set in the largest and northernmost of all the United States. Featuring an abundance of natural resources, beautiful landscapes and, if we're to believe everything on television (which we do), more men than anyone knows what to do with, Alaska is the perfect place to partner with a lumberjack to pan for gold or play in the snow.

MEN IN TREES
Elmo (fic.)   2006–2008
Famed author Marin Frist was so taken with the small-town charm of Elmo she uprooted her glamorous cosmopolitan life to move there. Catch her radio show on the local radio station.

NORTHERN EXPOSURE
Cicely (fic.)   1990–1995

If you're in Cicely, Alaska, be sure to stop by The Brick, the small town's most reliable restaurant. Owner Holling Vincoeur can be counted on to serve up some wisdom along with his signature dishes.

THE GOOD PLACE
2016–present

MEDIUM
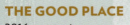
Phoenix   2005–2011

THE LYING GAME
Phoenix   2011–2013

PHOENIX

TUCSON

16

ARIZONA

Whether you're sitting on your backside on your recliner, or on an ass in The Grand Canyon, Arizona offers some quality programming choices. The Copper State offers enough gold-level sights and activities to turn your desert vacation into one awash in traditions and culture.

ALICE Phoenix 1976–1985

If you find yourself driving through Phoenix, be sure to stop by Mel's Diner, where the burgers are just okay, but the waitresses Alice, Flo, and Vera are a delight. You might even be invited to kiss Flo's "grits," wherever those are.

THE LAST MAN ON EARTH
Tucson 2015–2018
Just because you're traveling alone doesn't mean you can't have a great time in Arizona. From long walks to watching sunsets to wondering where everyone else is, you'll always find something to do when there's nobody to do it with.

TV USA
ARKANSAS

Home to the incomparable Crystal Bridges Museum of American Art, and home base of Walmart (where you may be thumbing through this book right now), Arkansas is the Jan Brady of all 50 states, being the 25th admitted to the Union. Any "Little Girl from Little Rock" can spend the day sitting on a porch watching its state insect, the honey bee, flitter around the garden, or turn around and watch the living room television through the window.

EVENING SHADE
Evening Shade (fic.)
1990–1994
Talk of the Evening Shade football team, coached by former Steelers player Wood Newton, dominates the porch conversations in this picturesque hamlet.

LITTLE ROCK

THE SIMPSONS
Springfield
1989–present

SUPERNATURAL
Little Rock   2005–present
If passing through Little Rock, you must plan a trip to the Arkansas Museum of Anthropology. Stuffed with enough treasures to fill your day, be sure to adhere to the posted times of operation as you are likely to be sent to nearby Green River County Detention Center should you be found there after hours.

THE ROCKFORD FILES
Malibu 1974–1980

If you find yourself in trouble, or the primary subject in a murder investigation, Malibu's Jim Rockford is the one to call. One of the few private investigators who still uses an answering machine, he's never had a disappointed client. Or girlfriend.

BIG LITTLE LIES Monterey 2017–present

Monterey has its share of natural wonders, but the local elementary school's annual musical, produced by alpha mom Madeline Martha Mackenzie rivals any sunrise or sunset found on the coast, or on Broadway.

ARRESTED DEVELOPMENT
Orange County 2003–2006; 2013–present

There's nothing more refreshing than a frozen banana on a hot day. Stop by Bluth's Original Frozen Banana stand, located on the pier and owned by the scions of the famed Bluth Company, for a tasty treat. You may even witness a few magic tricks!

SAN DIEGO

SIMON & SIMON 1981–1989

DRAKE & JOSH 2004–2007

THE GAME 2006–2015

THE FOSTERS 2013–2018

GRACE AND FRANKIE 2015–present

PITCH 2016

NED'S DECLASSIFIED SCHOOL SURVIVAL GUIDE
2004–2007

THE BIG VALLEY
Stockton
1965–1969

PETTICOAT JUNCTION
Hooterville & Pixley
1963–1970

MALIBU

DIAGNOSIS: MURDER 1993–2001

TWO AND A HALF MEN 2003–2015

ZOEY 101 2005–2008

HANNAH MONTANA 2006–2011

ALF San Fernando Valley 1986–1990
Despite frequent reports of alien behavior, and a shockingly high feline death rate, the San Fernando Valley is a great place to raise a family.

BASKETS Bakersfield 2016–present

SON OF ZORN
Orange County
2016–2017

HANGIN' WITH MR. COOPER
Oakland
1992–1997

S.W.A.T.
Southern California
1975–1976; revival 2017–present

THREE'S A CROWD
1984–1985

GIDGET
Southern California
1965–1966

STARSKY & HUTCH
Southern California
1975–1979

OAKLAND

STOCKTON

MONTEREY

PIXLEY

SAN FERNANDO VALLEY

BAKERSFIELD

MALIBU

ORANGE COUNTY

SOUTHERN CALIFORNIA

SAN DIEGO

THREE'S COMPANY San Diego 1977–1984
No need to knock on the door of the Regal Beagle. This always-open spot is perfect for lunch, dinner, or drinks, but be sure to be as clear and transparent as possible as misunderstandings happen with alarming frequency.

MR. SUNSHINE
San Diego 2011
Catch all the hottest events and bands at the Sunshine Center, San Diego's premiere arena.

MY THREE SONS Bryant Park (fic.) 1960–1972

THE MUNSTERS Mockingbird Heights (fic.) 1964–1966

THE PARTRIDGE FAMILY San Pueblo (fic.) 1970–1974

CHARLIE'S ANGELS 1976–1981; revival 2011

GIMME A BREAK! Glenlawn (fic.) 1981–1987

FIRST AND TEN 1984–1991

OUT OF THIS WORLD Marlowe (fic.) 1987–1991

BUFFY THE VAMPIRE SLAYER Sunnydale (fic.) 1996–2003

ROCKET POWER Ocean Shores (fic.) 1999–2004

GIRLFRIENDS 2000–2008

VERONICA MARS Neptune (fic.) 2004–2007

WEEDS Argestic (fic.) 2005–2012

SONS OF ANARCHY Charming (fic.) 2008–2014

TEEN WOLF Beacon Hills (fic.) 2011–2017

ARROW Starling City (fic.) 2012–present

FLAKED 2016–present

HEATHERS 2018–present

STAR TREK: VOYAGER
High Sierras 1995–2001
A beatiful spot for hiking, the High Sierras serve as the basis of one of computer pioneer Henry Starling's most fantastic stories of seeing a UFO from the future crash land.

IT'S GARRY SHANDLING'S SHOW
Sherman Oaks 1986–1990

THE BIG BANG THEORY
Pasadena 2007–present

JUST THE 10 OF US
Eureka
1988–1990

UNDECLARED
2001–2002

CHUCK
Burbank
2007–2012

FAMILY
Pasadena
1976–1980

PASADENA
Pasadena
2001

THE BEVERLY HILLBILLIES
Beverly Hills 1962–1971
While you're in Beverly Hills, make sure to take a bus ride that drives by the homes of the rich and famous. The most interesting home is owned by the Clampetts, recent transplants from the Deep South who've brought their Southern charm, and décor, with them.

90210
Beverly Hills 2008–2013

BEVERLY HILLS BUNTZ
Beverly Hills 1987–1988

BEVERLY HILLS 90210
Beverly Hills 1990–2000
In the mood for some comfort food? Try The Peach Pit, a local eatery favored by the popular kids. If you're around when the moon's out, try the adjacent Peach Pit After Dark nightclub, where you can see concerts given by the top recording artists of the day.

BAY CITY BLUES
Bay City 1983–1984

GETTING ON
Long Beach 2013–2015
If you're on the lookout for quality elder care, you could do better, *much* better, than the Billy Barnes Extended Care Unit of Mount Palms Memorial Hospital.

RAGS TO RICHES
Bel-Air 1987–1988

THE FRESH PRINCE OF BEL-AIR
Bel-Air 1990–1996

Map labels: EUREKA, HIGH SIERRAS, BAY CITY, BURBANK, SHERMAN OAKS, PASADENA, BEVERLY HILLS, LONG BEACH, BEL-AIR

STAR TREK: TNG Marin County **1987–1994**
Nestled on one side of the Golden Gate Bridge, Starfleet's training facility offers visitors a tour of the ships and technology of the future. Don't forget to trek to the gift shop!

SACRAMENTO

EIGHT IS ENOUGH 1977–1981

EVEN STEVENS 2000–2003

THE MENTALIST 2008–2015

SILICON VALLEY Silicon Valley **2014–present**
Home to more internet startups than are on the internet, including Pied Piper, Silicon Valley boasts one of the highest per capita net worths in the country.

PSYCH
Santa Barbara 2006–2014
You'll never have to worry about losing your keys in Santa Barbara, home to celebrity psychic and police consultant Shawn Spencer.

KNOTS LANDING Knots Landing (fic.) **1979–1993**

THE SIMPSONS
Springfield
1989–present

13 REASONS WHY
Northern California
2017–present

7TH HEAVEN
Glenoak (fic.)
1996–2007

MARIN COUNTY

SACRAMENTO

SILICON VALLEY

HOLLYWOOD

HAZEL 1961–1966

ACTION 1999–2000

GREG THE BUNNY 2002–2006

THE L WORD West Hollywood 2004–2009

HEAD CASE 2007–2009

VICTORIOUS 2010–2013

EPISODES 2011–2017

NOBODIES 2017–present

BLACK-ISH
Sherman Oaks
2014–present

GLENOAK

SHERMAN OAKS

HOLLYWOOD

SANTA BARBARA
Santa Barbara
1984–1993

SANTA BARBARA

SANTA CLARITA

PACIFIC PALASIDES

PALOS VERDE

RANCHO CUCAMONGA

SANTA CLARITA DIET
Santa Clarita 2017–present
Once you visit Santa Clarita, you'll want to live there! Call on local real estate agents Sheila and Joel Hammond for all your house-hunting needs.

WORKAHOLICS
Rancho Cucamonga
2011–2017

BORDERTOWN MEXIFORNIA
2016

SAVED BY THE BELL Pacific Palasides 1989–1993
There's something about California teens and their hangout restaurants. The kids from Bayside High gather at The Max, where you can find great eats and a blond guy breaking the Fourth Wall.

AWKWARD Palos Verde 2011–2016

MOM
Napa   2013–present
Napa is known for its wines, but if you're in recovery, Christy P. reports there are lots of Friends of Bill there, too.

THE FALL GUY
Hollywood   1981–1986

AMERICAN HORROR STORY 2011–present

THE ROOKIES 1972–1976

SONS AND DAUGHTERS 1974; revival 2006

MATT HOUSTON 1982–1985

REMINGTON STEELE 1982–1987

HIGHWAY TO HEAVEN 1984–1989

OUR HOUSE 1986–1988

NUMB3RS 2005–2010

GROWN-ISH 2018–present

THE PARKERS Santa Monica   1999–2004
Santa Monica Community College provides a quality eduction to traditional and non–traditional students alike. Check out Andell's restaurant, where all the cool kids hang out.

CRAZY EX-GIRLFRIEND
West Covina 2015–present
West Covina, located only two hours from the beach, is so lovely you're likely to break out into song.

PARENTHOOD
Berkeley 2010–2015

NAPA

BERKELEY

SAN JOSE

JUST OUR LUCK
Venice 1983

THE O.C.
Newport Beach
2003–2007
All of Newport Beach, if not the entire O.C., glows in the warmth of Christmas lights and Hanukkah candles as locals celebrate Christmukkah!

THE GOOD DOCTOR
San Jose
2017–present

THE ROPERS
Cheviot Hills
1979–1980

WEST COVINA

HOLLYWOOD

SANTA MONICA

CHEVIOT HILLS

ANIMAL KINGDOM
Oceanside
2016–present

GOLIATH
Santa Monica 2016–present

NEWPORT BEACH

VENICE

OCENSIDE

AMERICAN VANDAL
Oceanside & Carlsbad
2017–present

GOMER PYLE, USMC
Santa Monica 1964–1969

SAN DIEGO

IMPERIAL BEACH

MARCUS WELBY, M.D.
Santa Monica 1969–1976

THAT 80S SHOW
San Diego 2002

JOHN FROM CINCINNATI
Imperial Beach
2007

CALIFORNIA

LOS ANGELES

CHICO AND THE MAN
1974–1978
If you're having car trouble, stop by Ed Brown's Garage. Despite the rundown appearance, Ed and his mechanic, Chico, will get your car up and running in 22 minutes or less.

DRAGNET 1951–1959

COLUMBO 1968–2003

CANNON 1971–1976

BARNABY JONES 1973–1980

CHIPS 1977–1983

BJ AND THE BEAR 1979–1981

JAKE AND THE FATMAN 1987–1992

COP ROCK 1990

BAYWATCH NIGHTS 1995–1997

CYBILL 1995–1998

ANGEL 1999–2004

IT'S LIKE, YOU KNOW 1999–2000

JOEY 2004–2006

BROTHERS & SISTERS 2006–2011

CALIFORNICATION 2007–2014

CRASH 2008–2009

DOLLHOUSE 2009–2010

JONAS 2009–2010

BOSCH 2014–present

CODE BLACK 2015–2018

ALONE TOGETHER 2018

THE ROOKIE
2018–present

24
2001–2010; revival 2014

77 SUNSET STRIP
1958–1964

9-1-1
2018–present

BURKE'S LAW
1963–1966; revival 1994–1995

CURB YOUR ENTHUSIASM
2000–2011; revival 2017–present

ADAM-12
1968–1975; revival 1990–1991

SONNY WITH A CHANCE
2009–2011

MOONLIGHTING
1985–1989

BOJACK HORSEMAN
2014–present
If you're hungry enough to eat a horse, stop by Elefante, where Tinseltown's wildest flock and stampede to eat, see, and "bee" seen.

BAYWATCH
1989–2001
BAYWATCH NIGHTS
1995–1997
After spending the day in the sun and sand, check out Nights, a nightclub located a slow-motion run from the beach, for a supernaturally good time.

LOS ANGELES

THE LARRY SANDERS SHOW 1992–1998
Hey now—if you're in town and want to see a live taping, check out
The Larry Sanders Show, located in Hollywood. The studio is smaller
than you think it is, but the egos are bigger than you ever imagined.

HONEY WEST 1965–1966

HERE'S LUCY 1968–1974

EMERGENCY! 1972–1977

HART TO HART 1979–1984

HARDCASTLE & McCORMACK 1983–1986

HUNTER 1984–1991

L.A. LAW 1986–1994

GOING PLACES 1990–1991

GROSSE POINTE 2000–2001

GEORGE LOPEZ 2002–2007

HUFF 2004–2006

DROP DEAD DIVA 2009–2014

HAPPILY DIVORCED 2011–2013

HELLO LADIES 2013–2014

HIT THE FLOOR 2013–present

FEAR THE WALKING DEAD 2015–present

HEARTBEAT 2016

INSECURE 2016–present

LADY DYNAMITE 2016–2017

FAMOUS IN LOVE 2017–present

GLOW 2017–present

If you're traveling on a budget, and don't care about things like a full continental breakfast, check in to The Dusty Spur.

WHAT'S HAPPENING!!
1976–1979
WHAT'S HAPPENING NOW!!
1995–1998

For anything from burgers to fries to fries and burgers, stop by Rob's Place. Be prepared for long-time waitress Shirley to serve a slice of sass with your meal.

GIRLFRIEND'S GUIDE TO DIVORCE
2014–present

MACGYVER
1985–1992; revival 2016–present

KNIGHT RIDER
1982–1986; revival 2008–2009

MELROSE PLACE
1992–1999; revival 2009–2010

BIG TIME RUSH
2009–2013

IT'S A LIVING 1980–1989

Fine dining doesn't come any finer than dinner at Above the Top, where you'll be treated with amazing views of the LA skyline and the piano stylings of Sonny Mann. Be sure to be nice to hostess Nancy, or she'll sit you in Dot's section.

LOS ANGELES

BARRY 2018–present

The Lankershim Community Center provides Angelenos with a variety of classes, clinics, and cultural events. But as most everyone wants to be an actor, you can audit one of famed acting coach (and best-selling author of *Hit Your Mark and Say Your Lines*) Gene Cousineau's acting classes to learn how to kill it in your auditions.

THE MONKEES 1966–1968

MANNIX 1967–1975

THE MOD SQUAD 1968–1973

MEDICAL CENTER 1969–1976

THE WHITE SHADOW 1978–1981

THE CHARMINGS 1987–1988

MANN & MACHINE 1992

THE JAMIE FOXX SHOW 1996–2001

MOESHA 1996–2001

THE SHIELD 2002–2008

MOONLIGHT 2007–2008

MODERN FAMILY 2009–present

NCIS: LA 2009–present

LAW & ORDER: LA 2010–2011

MAJOR CRIMES 2012–2018

MARON 2013–2016

LIFE IN PIECES 2015–present

LUCIFER 2016–present

LINCOLN HEIGHTS 2007–2009

THE RUNAWAYS 2017–present

THE ADVENTURES OF OZZIE AND HARRIET
1952–1966

ANDI MACK
2017–present

LOU GRANT
1977–1982

DOOGIE HOWSER, M.D.
1989–1993

MODELS INC
1994–1995

SANFORD AND SON
1972–1977

POLICE STORY
1973–1979

YES, DEAR
2000–2006

THE SECRET LIFE OF THE AMERICAN TEENAGER
2008–2013

WISEGUY
1987–1990

SCORPION
2014–2018

ENTOURAGE   2004–2011
The entertainment's biggest stars, including *Aquaman* star Vincent Chase, can often be found taking a meeting at The Hollywood Roosevelt.

LOS ANGELES

THE BRADY BUNCH 1969–1974

George Glass reports that this Mike Brady–designed midcentury modern home in scenic North Hollwood, the subject of a recent bidding war, is home to not one but two musical acts: The Silver Platters and Johnny Bravo. If you play your cards right, you might even see today's hottest celebrites, like musical recording artist Davy Jones or famed quarterback Joe Namath, hanging around, too!

TOPPER 1953–1955

PERRY MASON 1957–1966

PETER GUNN 1958–1961

POLICE WOMAN 1974–1978

QUINCY, M.E. 1976–1983

TABITHA 1976–1978

THE BAD NEWS BEARS 1979–1980

THE GREATEST AMERICAN HERO 1981–1983

THE COLBYS 1985–1987

SIX FEET UNDER 2001–2005

THE CLOSER 2005–2012

THE COMEBACK 2005; revival 2014

NOAH'S ARC 2005–2006

PRIVATE PRACTICE 2007–2013

PARTY DOWN 2009–2010

RAY DONOVAN 2013–present

SCORPION 2014–2018

TRANSPARENT 2014–present

THE ARRANGEMENT 2017–2018

ONE DAY AT A TIME 2017–present

COBRA KAI Reseda 2018–present
Locals, especially teenagers, love taking classes at the Cobra Kai dojo in downton Reseda, where they put the philosophy of "Strike first. Strike hard. No mercy" into breaking boards.

VIDA
2018–present

NEW GIRL
2011–2018

TOGETHERNESS 2015–2016
If you're looking for a nonstop overseas voyage, board the SS *Tiptn*.

STUDIO 60 ON THE SUNSET STRIP 2006–2007
If comedy is your thing, line up early for a taping of NBS's *Studio 60*, the west coast's answer to NBC's *SNL*.

ELLEN 1994–1998
When visiting a new city, it's important to patronize small independent restaurants, shops, and especially bookstores, including Los Angeles's Buy the Book, owned by noted puppy enthusiast Ellen Morgan.

REAL HUSBANDS OF HOLLYWOOD
2013–2016

TRIAL & ERROR
1988

THE BIONIC WOMAN
1976–1978

SNOWFALL
2017–present

I'M DYING UP HERE
2017–present
Every upcoming comedian in The City of Angels angles for a spot on the stage at Goldies, a comedy club that has launched the careers of the best and brightest in entertainment.

YOU'RE THE WORST
2014–2018

THE BOLD AND THE BEAUTIFUL
1987–present

TV USA
CALIFORNIA
SAN FRANCISCO

SAN FRANCISCO

THE MAN IN THE HIGH CASTLE
2015–present

**HAVE GUN—
WILL TRAVEL**
1957–1963

MCMILLAN & WIFE 1971–1977

THE STREETS OF SAN FRANCISCO 1972–1977

ELI STONE 2008–2009

ACCIDENTALLY ON PURPOSE 2009–2010

LOOKING 2014–2016

YOUNG & HUNGRY 2014–2018

HOTEL 1983–1988
Owned by the aristocrat with Bette Davis eyes, Laura Trent, and managed by her equally regal sister-in-law, Victoria Cabot, The St. Gregory Hotel can't be beat for dramatic views, and encounters.

FULL HOUSE 1987–1995
There's so much to do in San Francisco, it's best to get the most up-to-date info by watching *Wake Up, San Francisco*, hosted by local dad Danny Tanner and his sister-in-law Becky Donaldson Katsopolis.

CHARMED 1998–2006; 2018–present
In the mood for some late night fun? Check out P3, owned and operated by local Piper Halliwell, where the drinks are so strong you'll swear you see people explode before your very eyes.

I REMEMER MAMA 1949–1957

IRONSIDE 1967–1975; revival 2013–2014

PHYLLIS 1975–1977

TRAPPER JOHN, M.D. 1979–1986

TOO CLOSE FOR COMFORT 1980–1987

MY SISTER SAM 1986–1988

HUMAN TARGET 1992; revival 2010–2011

TALES OF THE CITY 1993; 1998; 2001; 2019

ALL-AMERICAN GIRL 1994–1995

PARTY OF FIVE 1994–2000

SUDDENLY SUSAN 1996–2000

NASH BRIDGES 1996–2001

DHARMA AND GREG 1997–2002

BROTHER'S KEEPER 1998–1999

MONK 2002–2009

THAT'S SO RAVEN 2003–2007

THE BIONIC WOMAN 2007

FULLER HOUSE 2016–present

MAKE IT OR BREAK IT
Boulder 2009–2012

THE BILL ENGVALL SHOW
Louisville 2007–2009

LOUISVILLE

BOULDER

DENVER

ASCENSION

COLORADO SPRINGS

MORK & MINDY Denver 1978–1982
Shopping locally, especially in the music store owned by Denver Symphony Orchestra's Fred McConnell, will make you feel out of this world.

DR. QUINN, MEDICINE WOMAN
Colorado Springs 1993–1998
If you've made the arduous journey out West, and find yourself in need of windswept assistance, local handyman and ombre hombre Byron Sully can surely help with anything from repairing a loose wheel to repairing a broken heart.

STARGATE SG-1
Colorado Springs 1997–2007

THE SIMPSONS
Springfield 1989–present

TV USA

COLORADO

LAST MAN STANDING
Denver   2011–present

GOOD LUCK CHARLIE
Denver   2010–2014

COMMUNITY   Greendale (fic.)   2009–2015
Greendale Community College is known for many things, but a quality education is not necessarily one of them.

TOUCHED BY AN ANGEL
Ascension   1994–2003
The angels who work and live in and around Ascension are so nice you'll feel like you've died and gone to heaven.

THE RANCH   Garrison (fic.)   2016–present

EVERWOOD   Everwood (fic.)   2002–2006

KIM POSSIBLE   Middleton (fic.)   2002–2007

DYNASTY   Denver   1981–1989
If fireworks are your thing, check out any of the hundreds of charity balls attended by Krystle Carrington and her husband's ex-wife, Alexis Morell Carrington Colby Dexter Rowan.

AMERICAN HOUSEWIFE
Westport   2016–present

BEWITCHED   Westport   1964–1972
Try to ignore the ridiculous ramblings of local resident Gladys Kravitz, whose claims of witchcraft belong more in Salem than Westport, and enjoy the sights of this bedroom community just outside of New York.

HARTFORD

WESTPORT

FAIRFIELD

WHO'S THE BOSS?   Fairfield   1984–1992
Connecticut offers new beginnings and adventures for everyone, though sometimes the brand new life people find around the bend offers more question marks than expected.

SOAP
Dunn's River (fic.)   1977–1981

AS TOLD BY GINGER
Sheltered Shrubs (fic.)   2000–2016

CONNECTICUT

GILMORE GIRLS
Stars Hollow (fic.)
2000–2007; revival 2016
Enjoy a slow cup of coffee at Luke's Diner while eavesdropping on the locals speed-talking through every conversation.

JUDGING AMY   Hartford   1999–2005

TV USA
TV ROAD TRIP
QUANTUM LEAP • 1989–1993

If you ever look in the mirror and don't recognize yourself, it's time for a vacation. But make sure to keep grounded or you may never return home! Here are some places to check out before your plans are unexpectedly canceled:

1. "Genesis, Part 1": Edwards Air Force Base, Blockfield, CA

2. "Play It Again, Seymour": NYC, NY

3. "Southern Comforts": New Orleans, LA

4. "Leaping In Without A Net": near Denver, CO

5. "The Leap Home, Part 1": Elk Ridge, IN

6. "The Boogieman": Coventry, ME

7. "Runaway": Carbon County, WY

8. "Last Dance Before an Execution": Tallahassee, FL

9. "Unchained": Talawaga County, AL

10. "Mirror Image": Cokeburg, PA, and San Diego, CA

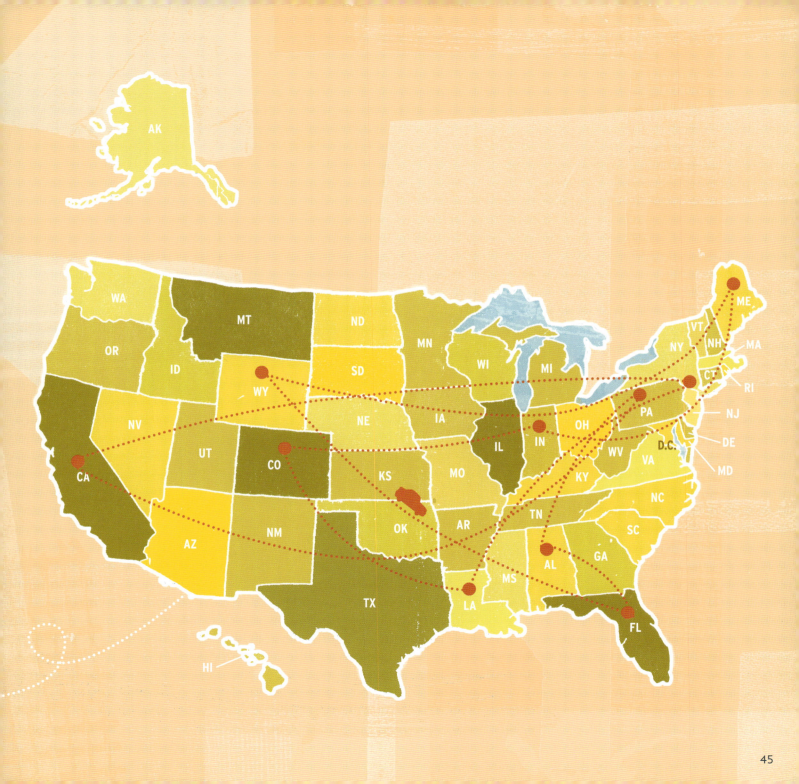

TV USA

DELAWARE

The First State may be last in number of settings for television shows, but that doesn't mean Delaware is any less important. Nicknamed "The Small Wonder," despite the fact that *Small Wonder* was probably set somewhere else, it has the lowest mean elevation of any state, but perhaps also the fewest mean people.

SMALL WONDER
1985–1989

THE PRETENDER
Blue Cove (fic.)   1996–2000
If you're in Delaware and need some help doing . . .
anything, there's someone to help you do everything.
In fact, it might be the same person.

TV USA
FLORIDA

COUGAR TOWN
Gulfhaven (fic.)   2009–2015

MIAMI

FLIPPER   1964–1967; revival 1995–2000

MIAMI VICE   1984–1990

EMPTY NEST   1988–1995

NURSES   1991–1994

THE GOLDEN PALACE   1992–1993

ODD MAN OUT   1999–2000

CSI: MIAMI   2002–2012

DEXTER   2006–2013

BURN NOTICE   2007–2013

AUSTIN & ALLY   2011–2016

MAGIC CITY   2012–2013

JANE THE VIRGIN   2014–present

BALLERS   2015–present

FRESH OFF THE BOAT
Orlando   2015–present
Locals and tourists alike love the western
flavors of Cattleman's Ranch, a steakhouse
featuring fresh flavors and boatloads of sides.

HOTWIVES OF ORLANDO
Orlando   2014–2015

SIT DOWN, SHUT UP
2009

GENTLE BEN
Florida Everglades   1967–1969

THE SIMPSONS
Springfield 1989–present

ENLISTED
Fort McGee (fic.) 2014

THE PAYNES
Sun Coast (fic.) 2018–present

I DREAM OF JEANNIE
Cocoa Beach 1965–1970

AMERICAN HORROR STORY
Jupiter 2011–present

COCOA BEACH

ORLANDO

PALMETTO

JUPITER

MIAMI

CLAWS Palmetto 2017–present
Treat yourself to the best manicure you'll ever have at Nail Artisans.
Just don't ask too many questions.

THE GOLDEN GIRLS
Miami 1985–1992
Any man traveling through Miami owes it to himself to stop by the museum. Not for the art, but to meet administrator Blanche Deveraux. Trust us.

BLOODLINE
2015–2017

49

TV USA

GEORGIA

DESIGNING WOMEN Atlanta 1986–1993
If you're looking to freshen up your point of view, you cannot do better than stopping by Sugarbaker & Associates, where, if you're lucky, you'll receive a complimentary soliloquy along with your design consultation.

ATLANTA
Atlanta 2016–present
Atlanta is the place to discover upcoming musical artists, like hometown hip-hop star Paper Boi, who can still be seen out and about.

ATLANTA

MATLOCK 1986–1995

PROFILER 1996–2000

TYLER PERRY'S HOUSE OF PAYNE 2007–2012

TYLER PERRY'S MEET THE BROWNS 2009–2011

THE WALKING DEAD 2010–present

SINGLE LADIES 2011–2015

SURVIVOR'S REMORSE 2014–2017

STAR 2016–present

DYNASTY (REVIVAL) 2017–present

THE MISADVENTURES OF SHERIFF LOBO
Orly County (fic.) 1979–1981

THE SIMPSONS
Springfield 1989–present

MEET THE BROWNS
Decatur 2009–2011

ATLANTA

DECATUR

SAVANNAH
Savannah 1996–1997

SAVANNAH

**THE HAVES AND
THE HAVE NOTS**
Savannah 2013–present
Try crashing one of the
galas hosted by local grand
dame Katheryn Cryer, if
you have the inclination and
have not already.

THE DUKES OF HAZZARD
Hazard County (fic.) 1979–1985

HAWAII

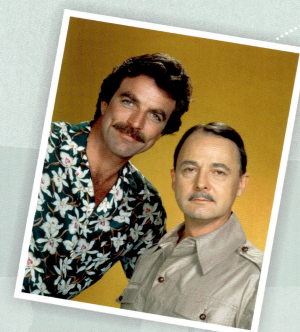

MAGNUM, P.I.
1980–1988; revival 2018–present
If you're looking for a fun and informative way to see the best of all of the Hawaiian islands, charter a helicopter flight from "Island Hoppers," owned and operated by local businessman and Vietnam vet Theodore "T.C." Calvin.

GILLIGAN'S ISLAND
Honolulu   1964–1967
Southampton, England, may have its Titanic, but Americans can pay their respects in Honolulu, where The Minnow departed and never returned from a three-hour tour. A three-hour tour.

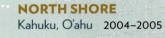

KAHUKU, O'AHU

HONOLULU

HAWAII FIVE-O
1968–1980; revival 2010–present
Local entrepeneaur Kamekona Tupuola's two
food trucks, Wailola Shave Ice and Kamekona's
Shrimp Truck, have been providing locals and
tourists authentic Hawaiin flavors for years.

LILO & STITCH: THE SERIES
2003–2006

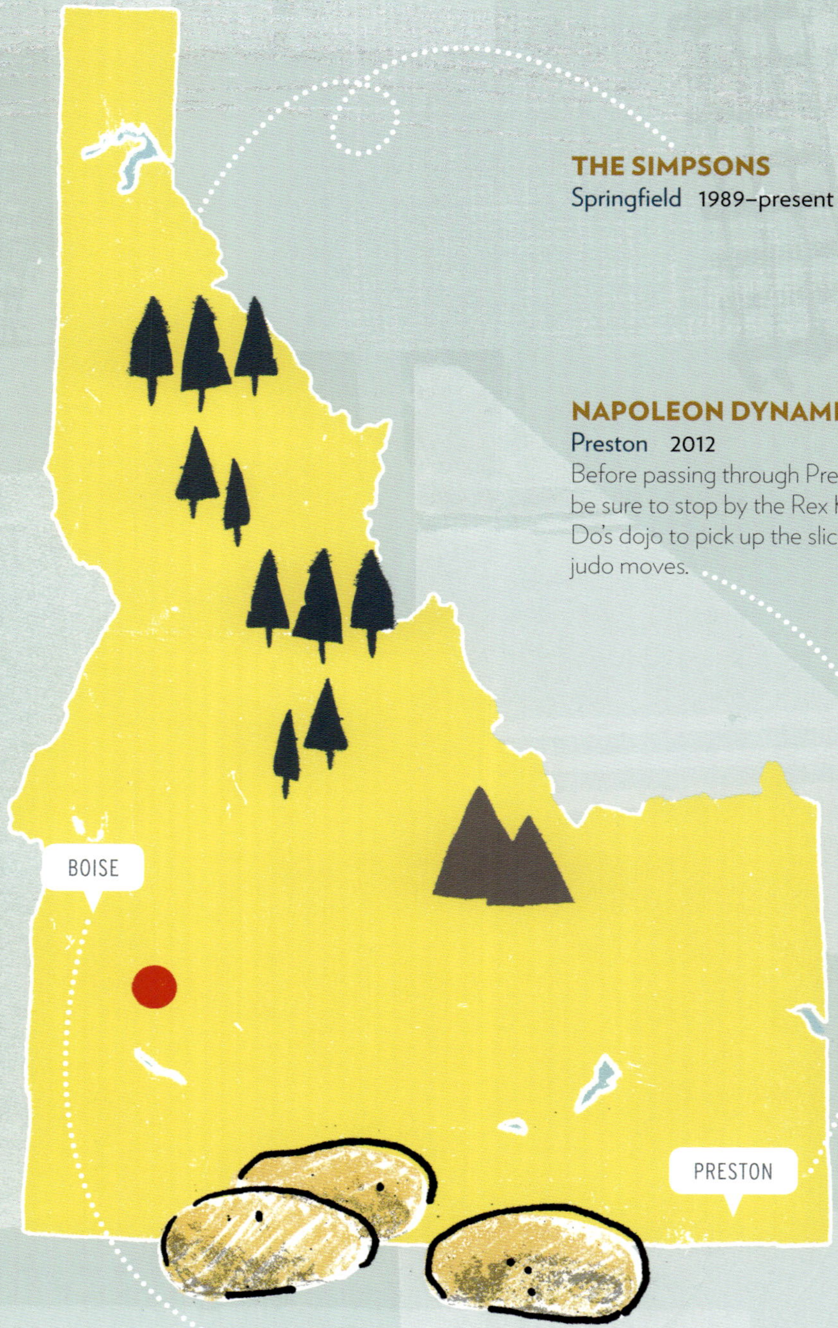

THE SIMPSONS
Springfield 1989–present

NAPOLEON DYNAMITE
Preston 2012
Before passing through Preston, be sure to stop by the Rex Kwon Do's dojo to pick up the slickest judo moves.

BOISE

PRESTON

TV USA
IDAHO

Whether on potatoes or people, all of the eyes in Idaho are peeled (literally and figuratively) to screens every night watching the fine programming offered by various providers (including broadcast television, if that still exists when you read this) in not one but two time zones. So whether you're on Mountain or Pacific, it's always prime time in the Gem State.

THE GRINDER
Boise   2015–2016
The law firm of Sanderson & Yao is staffed with gifted lawyers, but even if you don't need legal representation, it's still fun to make an appointment with TV's "Mitch Grinder," Dean Sanderson!

TV USA

ILLINOIS

THE SIMPSONS
Springfield 1989–present

VALERIE
VALERIE'S FAMILY
THE HOGAN FAMILY
Oak Park 1986–1991

ROSEANNE
Lanford 1988–1997; revival 2018

THE CONNERS
Lanford 2018–present

PERFECT STRANGERS
Chicago 1986–1993
The Ritz Discount store offers consumers
a wide range of products at rock-
bottom prices.

THE BOONDOCKS
Woodcrest (fic.) 2005–2014

AS THE WORLD TURNS
Oakdale (fic.) 1956–2010

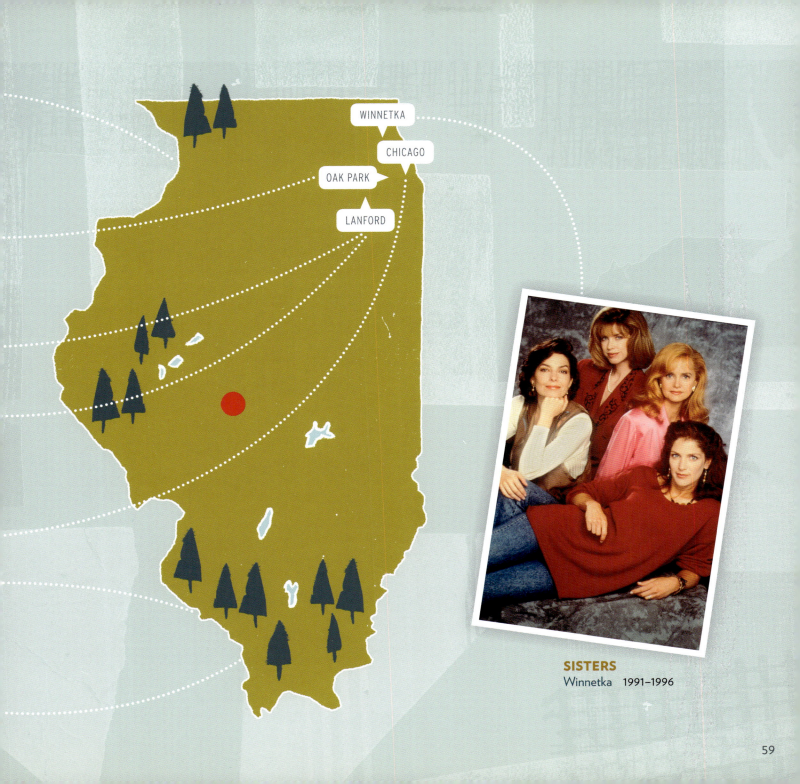

WINNETKA

CHICAGO

OAK PARK

LANFORD

SISTERS
Winnetka   1991–1996

CHICAGO

THE UNTOUCHABLES
1959–1963; revival 1993–1994

THE BOB NEWHART SHOW 1972–1978

GOOD TIMES 1974–1980

KOLCHAK: THE NIGHT STALKER
1974–1975

IT TAKES TWO 1982–1983

JOANIE LOVES CHACHI 1982–1983

WEBSTER 1983–1987

PUNKY BREWSTER 1984–1988

FAMILY MATTERS 1989–1998

FATHER DOWLING MYSTERIES 1989–1991

LIFE GOES ON 1989–1993

CHICAGO HOPE 1994–2000

EARLY EDITION 1996–2000

THE PJS 1999–2001

SOUL FOOD 2000–2004

ACCORDING TO JIM 2001–2009

KENAN & KEL 1996–2001
If you're looking for a great burger and a great insight into the tween mind, stop in to Chicago's Good Burger.

ER 1994–2009

MARRIED...
WITH CHILDREN 1987–1997
If you find yourself in the need of last-minute wardrobe help, there are lots of places other than Gary's Shoes and Accessories for Today's Woman. Seriously, go anywhere else.

CHICAGO

STILL STANDING   2002–2006

MY BOYS   2006–2010

THE LEAGUE   2009–2015

MIKE & MOLLY   2010–2016

SHAKE IT UP   2010–2013

BOSS   2011–2012

CHICAGO FIRE   2012–present

CHICAGO PD   2014–present

SIRENS   2014–2015

CHICAGO MED   2015–present

TEACHERS   2016–present

CHICAGO JUSTICE   2017

THE GOOD FIGHT   2017–present

RAVEN'S HOME   2017–present

THE CHI   2018–present

ANYTHING BUT LOVE
1989–1992
For info on the coolest things to do and see in Chicago, check out *Chicago Weekly*.

HAPPY ENDINGS 2011–2013
Chicago is home to some of the best food trucks in the country. Be sure to try Steak Me Home Tonight for some good food and, if you're lucky, a serenade by owner and chef Dave Rose.

THE GOOD WIFE
2009–2016

SUPERIOR DONUTS 2017–2018
There's nothing quite like the atmostphere and flavors found in local donut shops. Check out Superior Donuts, owned by Chicago's own Arthur Przybyszewski, for some sweet treats and some sour glances.

SHAMELESS 2011–present

THE SIMPSONS
Springfield   1989–present

THE MIDDLE
Orson (fic.)   2009–2018

INDIANAPOLIS

BLOOMINGTON

ONE DAY AT A TIME
Indianapolis   1975–1984
Somewhere there's music playing,
maybe at Indianapolis's premiere
PR firm, Connors & Davenport!

BREAKING AWAY
Bloomington   1980–1981

TV USA

INDIANA

THE JEFF FOXWORTHY SHOW
Bloomington   1995–1997

EERIE, IN   Eerie (fic.)   1991–1992
With a population of 1,661, Eerie, Indiana may not be the biggest town, but it's certainly one of the more . . . interesting ones.

PARKS AND RECREATION
Pawnee (fic.)   2009–2015
Take a break from exploring Pawnee's beautiful parks and stop by JJ's Diner for a waffle, or something, but nothing's as good as their waffles.

STRANGER THINGS
Hawkins (fic.)   2016–present
Whether you're looking for school supplies or even off-season Christmas lights, Melvald's General Store is the place for anything you need in Hawkins, IN.

TV USA

IOWA

DOUBLE TROUBLE
Des Moines   1984–1985
Des Moines is home to many cultural events but none as important as the Channel 62 Dance Contest where you, or your identical twin sister, can be propelled from anonymity to infamy in one aerobic jump.

PLYMOUTH COUNTY

DAMNATION
Plymouth County   2017–2018
You may have to cross a picket line or know the password to find some of Holden County's most interesting treasures, including its famously infamous speakeasy. For other entertainments, ask for Bessie.

THE SIMPSONS
Springfield   1989–present

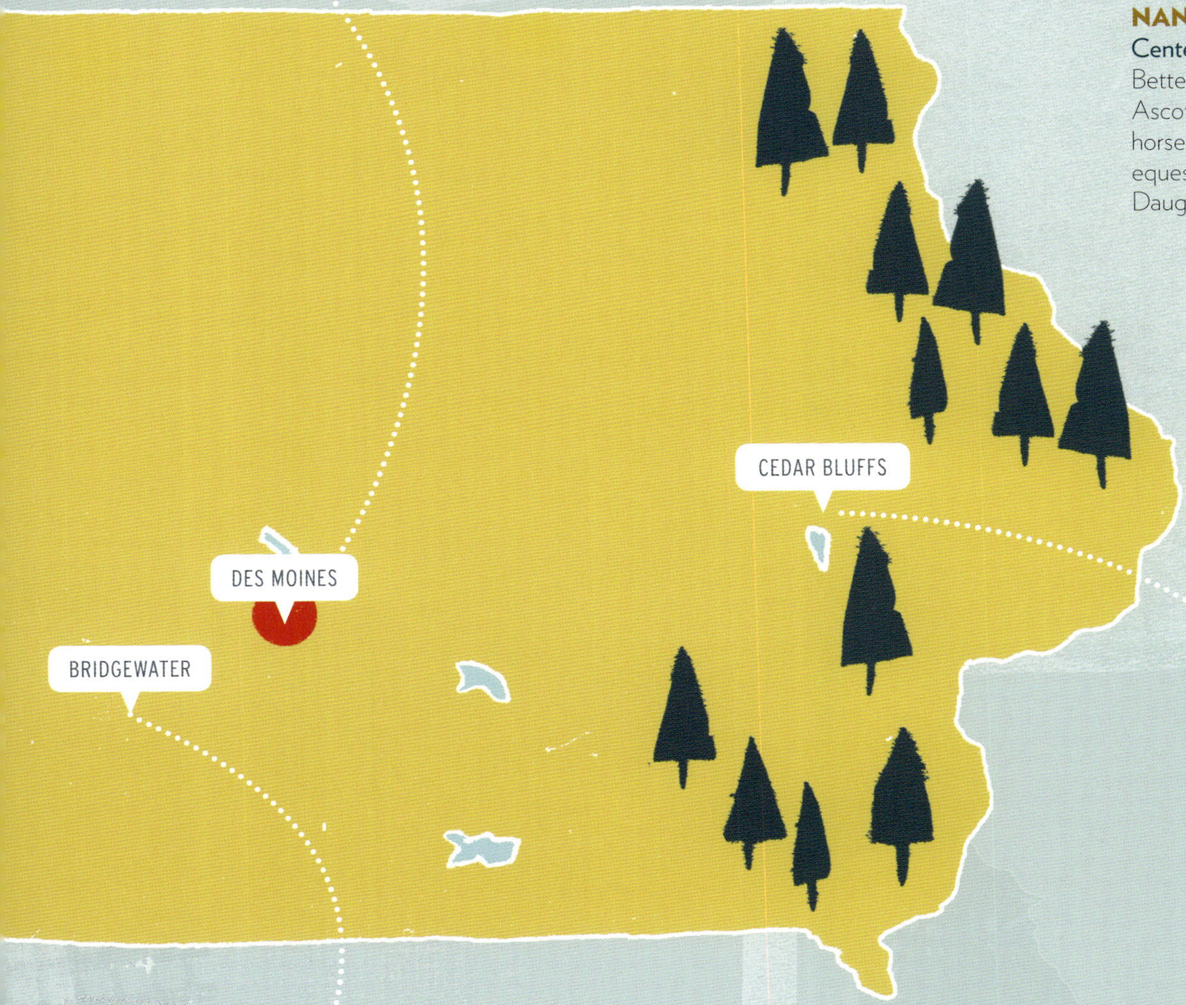

NANCY
Center City (fic.) 1970–1971
Better than the stuffy Royal Ascot races, Center City's annual horse show attracts hundreds of equestrians, breeders, and First Daughters each year.

CEDAR BLUFFS

DES MOINES

BRIDGEWATER

RUNAWAY
Bridgewater 2006
If you're looking for a place to escape your worries, you can't do better than Bridgewater, Iowa. Filled with houses that look exactly the same, your troubles, or killers, will have a really hard time finding you!

DREXEL'S CLASS
Cedar Bluffs 1991–1992

GUNSMOKE
Dodge City 1955–1975
If you're in the mood to whet your whistle (or anything else), make a stop at the Long Branch Saloon. There, Miss Kitty will bend over backward to make sure you leave satisfied.

ELLSWORTH

DODGE CITY

DENNIS THE MENACE
Wichita 1959–1963; animated series 1986–1988

THE PHIL SILVERS SHOW
Roseville (fic.)   1955–1959

OVERLAND PARK

WICHITA

SMALLVILLE
Smallville (fic.)   2001–2011

JERICHO
Jericho (fic.)   2006–2008

UNITED STATES OF TARA
Overland Park   2009–2011
Overland Park has something for everyone, or something for everyone you are that day.

THE LIFE AND LEGEND OF WYATT EARP
Ellsworth and Wichita   1955–1961

69

TV ROAD TRIP

THE X-FILES • 1993–2002

Everyone needs a vacation, and though it's hard to find the time, you need to put down those files of papers, walk out of your office, and go outside and relax. The truth of it is, it's out there. The following are but some of the spots to mark your own "eXperience":

1. "Ice": AK

2. "Drive": Buhl, ID, and Elko, NV

3. "Clyde Bruckman's Final Repose": St. Paul, MN

4. "Home": Home, PA

5. "Kaddish": Brooklyn, NY

6. "The Post-Modern Prometheus": Albion, IN

7. "Bad Blood": Chaney, TX

8. "Jose Chung's From Outer Space": Klass County, WA

9. "The Jersey Devil": Atlantic City, NJ

10. Pilot: Bellefleur, OR, and Washington, D.C.

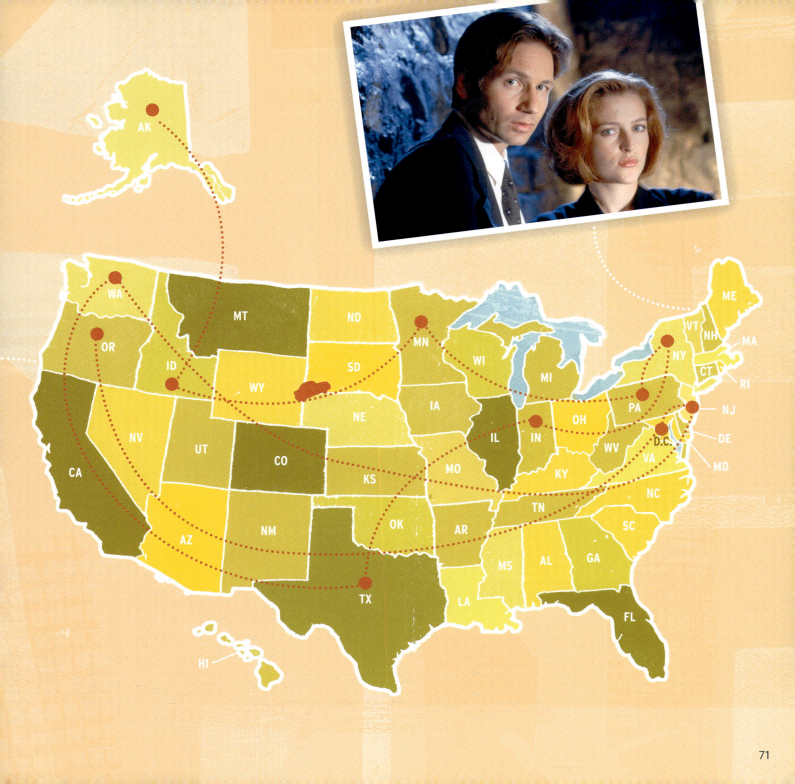

KENTUCKY

You may know about Kentucky from television commercials featuring the Colonel, but the Bluegrass State is so much more than a bucket of chicken. You can count cash at Fort Knox, and your blessings, when you visit and find "My Old Kentucky Home" will be yours as well.

THE SIMPSONS
Springfield 1989–present

AMERICAN GODS   2017–present

Anyone who's anyone attends the annual Easter banquet thrown at one of Kentucky's most luxurious, and rabbbit–filled, estates. You'll thank the gods for your invitation!

JUSTIFIED   Harlan   2010–2015

Your visit to Harlan, and nearby Noble's Hollow, will be justified if you stop by Ellstin Limehouse's diner, where you'll enjoy the freshest cuts of meat you've ever tasted.

HARLAN

LOUISIANA

TRUE DETECTIVE
2014–present

TREME Treme 2010–2013
Located in the Treme neighborhood of New Orleans, Janette Desautel's restaurant came back from Hurricane Katrina to serve locals and tourists some of the best food the Crescent City has to offer.

NEW ORLEANS

BOURBON STREET BEAT 1959–1960

THE ORIGINALS 2013–2018

NCIS: NEW ORLEANS 2014–present

QUEEN SUGAR 2016–present

CLOAK AND DAGGER 2018–present

AMERICAN HORROR STORY
New Orleans 2011–present

TRUE BLOOD Bon Temps 2008–2014
You can really sink your teeth into the fare served up at Merlotte's. Perfect for locals but welcoming to anyone passing through day (and especially night).

BON TEMPS

NEW ORLEANS

TREME

THE SIMPSONS
Springfield 1989–present

ONCE UPON A TIME
Story Brooke (fic.)   2011–2018

THE MIST
Bridgeville (fic.)
2017

HAVEN   Haven (fic.)
2010–2015

THE SIMPSONS
Springfield   1989–present

WATERVILLE

CASTLE ROCK

THE GHOST & MRS. MUIR
Schooner Bay (fic.)   1968–1970

CASTLE ROCK
Castle Rock   2018
The sun may not always be shining in Castle Rock, and it's often a dead zone for cell service, but located near Salem's Lot and Shawshank State Penitentiary it is, nevertheless, a place to find your needful things.

TV USA

MAINE

DARK SHADOWS
Collinsport (fic.)   1966–1971; revival 1991

WET HOT AMERICAN SUMMER
Waterville   2015 & 2017
Kids can't wait to return to Camp Firewood
every summer. There, they experience the
best Maine has to offer, in addition to learning
about birds, bees, and asteroids.

TV USA
MARYLAND

Like a cable box offering a never-ending variety of programming, the state nicknamed "Little America" contains a multitude of options for any tourist. From marshlands to mountains, from family comedy to gritty drama, Maryland is much more than a suburb of Washington, D.C.

THE WIRE
Baltimore 2002–2008
Baltimore is a city filled with contradictions and activities. For the most accurate and up-to-date information regarding the goings-on, including the hottest restaurants, check out the listings and reviews in *The Baltimore Sun*, the city's go-to resource for all cultural events.

BALTIMORE

ROC 1991–1994

HOMICIDE: LIFE ON THE STREET 1993–1999

ONE ON ONE 2001–2006

BALTIMORE

CHESAPEAKE SHORES
Chesapeake Shores (fic.)
2016–present
Chesapeake Shores is the perfect destination if you're in the mood for a weekend or overnight getaway. Check in to the Inn at Eagle Point for a cozy night or two.

TV USA
MASSACHUSETTS

AMERICAN HORROR STORY
2011–present

BOSTON

BANACEK 1972–1974

THE PRACTICE 1976–1977

CHEERS 1982–1993

ST. ELSEWHERE 1982–1988

SPENSER: FOR HIRE 1985–1988

BOSTON COMMON 1996–1997

ALLY MCBEAL 1997–2002

BOSTON PUBLIC 2000–2004

CROSSING JORDAN 2001–2007

BOSTON LEGAL 2004–2008

FRINGE 2008–2013

STUCK IN THE MIDDLE 2016–2018

SMILF 2017–present

SABRINA, THE TEENAGE WITCH
Westbridge (fic.) 1996–2003

THE SIMPSONS
Springfield 1989–present

WINGS
Nantucket 1990–1997
It can be tricky getting on and off an island as small as Nantucket, but both Sandpiper Air and Aeromass offer daily flights to and from Tom Nevers Field.

BOSTON

NANTUCKET

DAWSON'S CREEK
Capeside (fic.) 1998–2003
Capeside, MA, is beautiful any time of year, but for a real treat, take a canoe or rowboat along its famed creek to soak up the visual beauty and drama found along its shores.

SOMERSET
Somerset (fic.)   1970–1976

ASH VS EVIL DEAD
2015–2018

FREAKS AND GEEKS   Chippewa   1999–2000
For a small town, Chippewa has a vibrant nightlife. Local bands Dimension and Feedback perform regularly at no-cover bars, and shouldn't be missed.

CHIPPEWA

AMERICAN HORROR STORY
Brookfield Heights (fic.)   2011–present

BAY CITY

DETROIT

MARTIN   Detroit   1992–1997
Detroit's own Martin Payne hosts a public access show where he talks about everything from current events to the must-dos-and-sees in the Motor City.

MICHIGAN

ANOTHER WORLD
Bay City   1964–1999
The home of Cory Publishing, parent company of *Brava* magazine, Bay City has everything you're looking for in a small city, including glamour, top-notch-hospitals, other-side-of-the-tracks drama, and enough intrigue to satisfy you and your evil never-before-seen twin.

DETROIT

SISTER, SISTER   1994–1999

8 SIMPLE RULES   2002–2005

BLADE: THE SERIES   2006

HUNG   2009–2011

GOOD GIRLS   2018–present

THE SIMPLONS
THE SIMPSONS
Springfield   1989–present

BUNK'D
Moose Rump (fic.)   2015–2018

HOME IMPROVEMENT   Detroit   1991–1999
Detroit's a great place for local television. If you're looking for some suburban comfort food, check out Tool Time, hosted by Tim Taylor, to learn all about how to improve your home.

TV USA
MINNESOTA

COACH 1989–1997

Though about 60% of Minnesota's population lives in the Minneapolis–Saint Paul area, 100% of all visitors are guaranteed a good time in The Land of 10,000 Lakes. Whether you're enjoying the sights on a hike, or watching television while recovering from a hike in Rochester's Mayo Clinic, there are more things to do and see than there are snowflakes in a blizzard.

LITTLE HOUSE ON THE PRAIRIE
Walnut Grove   1974–1983
A bit old-fashioned and a little overpriced, you can find everything you need at Oleson's General Store.

THE SIMPSONS
Springfield 1989–present

FARGO
Bemidji 2014–present
Stop by Lou's Coffee Shop for a
warm cup of joe on a freezing day.

THE BIG C
Minneapolis 2010–2013

BEMIDJI

MINNEAPOLIS

WALNUT GROVE

ST. PAUL

THE MARY TYLER MOORE SHOW
Minneapolis 1970–1977
Minneapolis has much more to offer than
The Mall of America. Be sure to start your
days watching WJM for the latest news and
events.

GET A LIFE
St. Paul 1990–1992

TV USA

MISSISSIPPI

Mississippi may have more letters than TV, but it's just as rich in options for tourists. Birthplace of Fred Armisen, who's probably starring in the show you're watching right now, my favorite Ray Walston, and once and again, Sela Ward, The Magnolia State is overflowing with music venues, historic sites, and outdoor activities.

ONE MISSISSIPPI
Bay St. Lucille (fic.)   2015–2017
One of the highlights of the year is Bay St. Lucille's annual Civil War reenactment. Drawing participants from across the state, locals and visitors alike take great pleasure, and pride, in their faithful recreation of the War Between the States.

IN THE HEAT OF THE NIGHT
Sparta (fic.)   **1988–1995**
Day or night, Joanne St. John's "Magnolia Café" offers up the best southern fare in Mississippi.

TV USA
MISSOURI

MAMA'S FAMILY Raytown 1983–1990
Filled with midwestern charms, local, family-owned businesses like Ed's Hardware Store make Raytown a lovely, wholesome place to raise any family.

SUPERSTORE
St. Louis   2015–present
Though there's probably one in your home town, the St. Louis branch of Cloud Nine often offers customers deep discounts based on damage caused by its employees' shenanigans. Be sure to listen for announcements as you may get some gossip along with your bargains.

SWITCHED AT BIRTH
Kansas City   2011–2017

GRACE UNDER FIRE
1993–1998

AFTER MASH
Riverbend (fic.)   1983–1985

THE FLASH
Central City (fic.)   2014–present

THE SIMPSONS
Springfield   1989–present

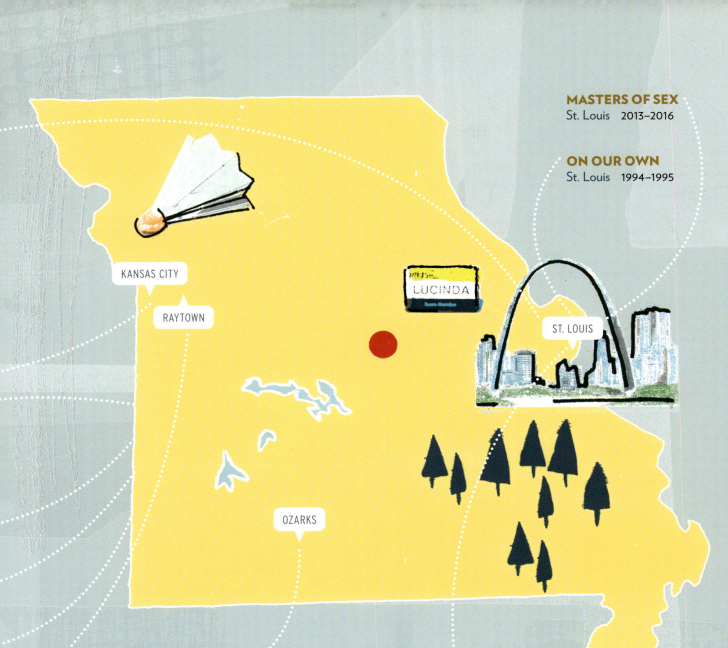

MASTERS OF SEX
St. Louis   2013–2016

ON OUR OWN
St. Louis   1994–1995

KANSAS CITY

RAYTOWN

LUCINDA

ST. LOUIS

OZARKS

OZARK Ozarks 2017–present
Though the Ozarks attract an enormous number of visitors during the summer months, locals and transplants from the big city enjoy the sleepy charms all year long. Lots of mom-and-pop stores, including markets, clubs, and laundry services are available.

THE SOUL MAN
St. Louis   2012–2016
If you're in St. Louis on Christmas, Easter, or just a Sunday, you'll be welcomed in Reverend Sherman Boyce "The Voice" Ballentine's church, where he serves up some soul for your soul.

You may not find a lot of shows when touring Big Sky Country, but regardless of which side of the Continental Divide you find yourself, you only need to look up to find more stars than there are on television.

HELL ON WHEELS 2011–2016

DIRK GENTLY'S HOLISTIC DETECTIVE AGENCY

Bergsberg (fic.)   2016–2017

If you're trying to figure out how everything is connected, contact Dirk Gently for answers. Confusing answers, but answers nonetheless.

TV ROAD TRIP

SUPERNATURAL • 2005–PRESENT

There's nothing more magical than the natural sights and sounds found in The United States. Whether you're traveling on your own, with family, or with friends, you'll always have an angel on your shoulder to guarantee a super time! Here are some suggestions for your wayward travels:

1. Pilot: Lawrence, KS

2. "Bloody Mary": Toledo, OH

3. "Weekend at Bobby's": Kenosha, WI

4. "Dead Man's Blood": Pueblo, CO

5. "Crossroad Blues": MS

6. "All Dogs Go to Heaven": Buffalo, NY

7. "Devil May Care": Eugene, OR

8. "The Girl Next Door": MT

9. "Rock and a Hard Place": Sioux Falls, SD

10. "Black": Beulah, ND

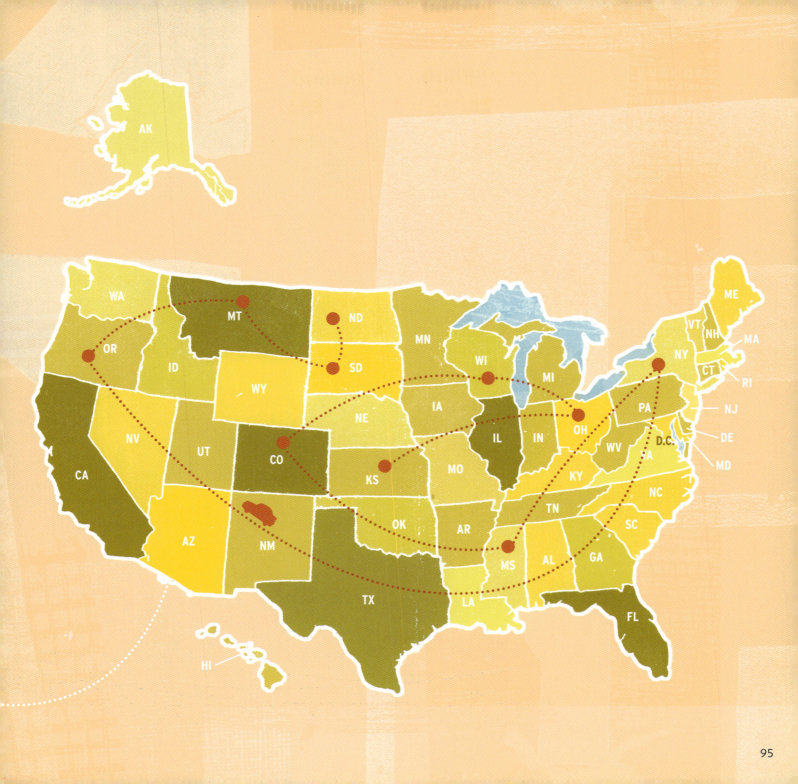

TV USA
NEBRASKA

Some people, especially those who keep their eyes trained on their seat-back monitors, consider Nebraska to be just a fly-over state. But if they took the time to get off the airplane, they'd see a vacation's worth of possibilities.

STAR TREK
Omaha   1966–1969
Take a tour of Offutt Air Force Base where, aside from seeing new and classic planes and equipment, you'll be treated to hearing about the mystery surrounding Captain John Christopher, who disappeared for some time in 1969. Some say he was kidnapped by a UFO sent by men from the future, but Christopher, whose son Colonel Shaun Geoffrey Christopher famously manned the first mission to Saturn, has never spoken of it.

THE SIMPSONS
Springfield 1989–present

RACHEL GUNN, R.N.
1992

THE YOUNG RIDERS
Sweetwater 1989–1992

SWEETWATER

OMAHA

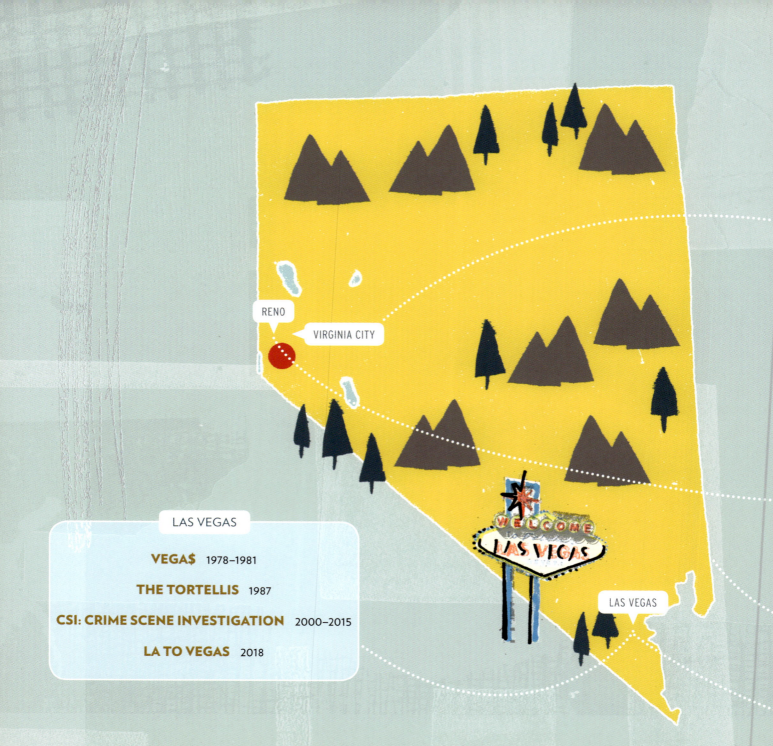

RENO

VIRGINIA CITY

LAS VEGAS

LAS VEGAS

VEGA$ 1978–1981

THE TORTELLIS 1987

CSI: CRIME SCENE INVESTIGATION 2000–2015

LA TO VEGAS 2018

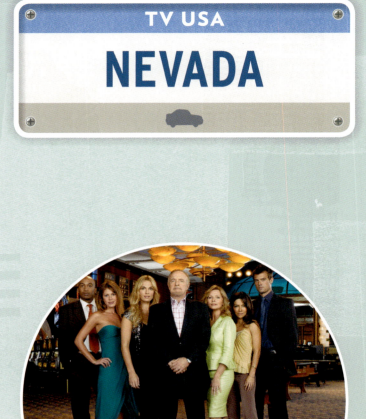

BONANZA Virginia City 1959–1973
The Comstock Silver Lodge is the perfect place to stay when touring the mines of the famed Comstock Silver Lode. You'll get an eyeful of precious metals and the virile young men who work the land of the neighboring ranch.

RENO 911! Reno 2003–2009
Many visitors wish to memorialize their time in Reno by getting a tattoo. We suggest that unless you wish to be filmed and/or disappointed, you avoid Ron's Tattoo Parlor at all costs.

SHE'S THE SHERIFF
Lakes County (fic.) 1987–1989

LAS VEGAS Las Vegas 2003–2008
High rollers and locals love the action and ambience at The Montecito Resort and Casino, where you can eat, drink, gamble, or just watch the beautiful people do beautiful things beautifully.

TV USA

NEW HAMPSHIRE

With a motto like "Live Free or Die," you'd expect New Hampshirites to balk at paying for cable, but The Old Man in the Mountain may be the only Granite Stater who relies solely on broadcast television.

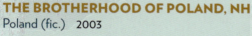

THE BROTHERHOOD OF POLAND, NH
Poland (fic.)   2003

STAN AGAINST EVIL
Willard's Mill (fic.)   2016–present
Willard's Mill's most popular and exclusive social group, The Black Hat Society, meets regularly to plan upcoming events and activities.

ICHABOD AND ME
Phippsborough (fic.)   1961–1962

THE SIMPSONS
Springfield   1989–present

TV USA
NEW JERSEY

THE SIMPSONS
Springfield   1989–present

New Jersey is more than just diners and malls (though it does have one of the highest per-capita numbers of each). The Garden State is replete with farmers' markets, quaint towns, and bustling metro areas that make every episode an interesting and entertaining tour du force right before you call it a day and suddenly fade to bla--.

THE SOPRANOS
Elizabeth   1999–2007
For the best Italian food you've ever eaten, try Nuovo Vesuvio.

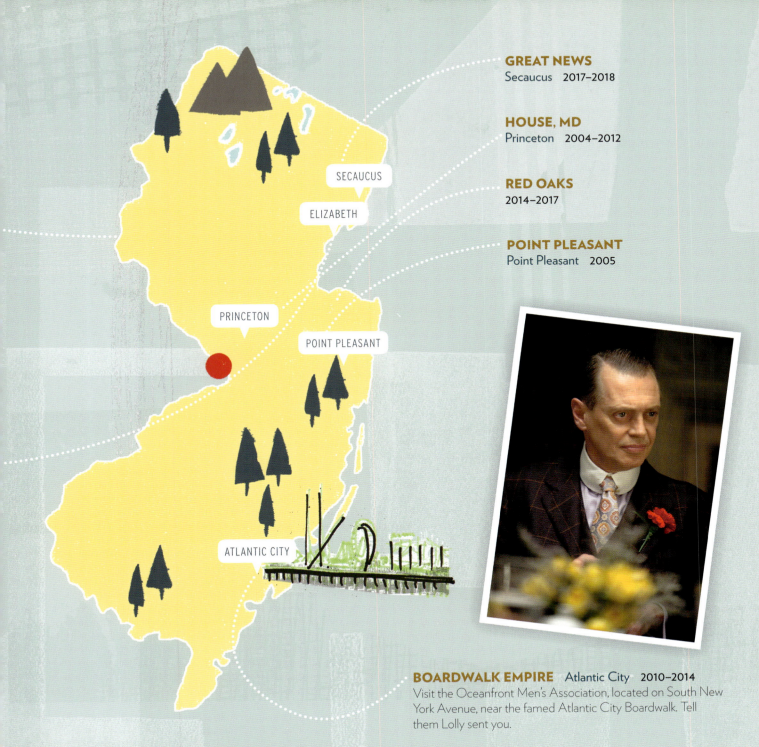

GREAT NEWS
Secaucus   2017–2018

HOUSE, MD
Princeton   2004–2012

RED OAKS
2014–2017

POINT PLEASANT
Point Pleasant   2005

SECAUCUS

ELIZABETH

PRINCETON

POINT PLEASANT

ATLANTIC CITY

BOARDWALK EMPIRE   Atlantic City   2010–2014
Visit the Oceanfront Men's Association, located on South New York Avenue, near the famed Atlantic City Boardwalk. Tell them Lolly sent you.

TV USA
NEW MEXICO

BREAKING BAD
Albuquerque   2008–2013
You can't beat Los Pollos Hermanos for quick, inexpensive Mexican food.

ROSWELL   Roswell   1999–2002; revival 2018
The Crashdown Café, owned and operated by Jeff Parker, is the go-to spot for a quick bite or spotting locals, some of whom moved there from quite far away.

STAR TREK: DS9   Roswell   1993–1999
Long rumored to be the site of a 1947 encounter with aliens, but definitely the site of a nuclear test, Roswell's army base offers anyone an otherworldly experience for those who wish to boldly go there.

BETTER CALL SAUL
Albuquerque   2015–present

THE RIFLEMAN
North Folk (fic.)   1958–1963

ALBUQUERQUE

ROSWELL

QUANTUM LEAP
1989–1993

105

NEW YORK

WONDERFALLS Niagara Falls 2004

WILL & GRACE
New York City 1998–2006; revival 2017–present
For a gay ol' time just stop by the Duplex in
Greenwich Village, a two story bar that
hosts some of the best singalongs and
performance artists.

I LOVE LUCY
Manhattan and upstate
1951–1957

GENERAL HOSPITAL Port Charles 1963–present

THE COMMISH Eastbridge 1991–1996

PORT CHARLES Port Charles (fic.) 1997–2003

TWISTED Green Grove (fic.) 2013–2014

GOTHAM Gotham (fic.) 2014–present

THE LEFTOVERS Mapleton (fic.) 2014–2017

BOB'S BURGERS Long Island 2011–present

GROWING PAINS Huntington, Long Island 1985–1992

THE SIMPSONS
Springfield 1989–present

GLORIA
Fox Ridge 1982–1983

THE ADVENTURES OF PETE & PETE
Wellsville 1991–1996

ORANGE IS THE NEW BLACK
Upstate New York 2013–present

DIVORCE
Hastings-on-Hudson 2016–present

THE FACTS OF LIFE
Peekskill 1979–1988

MAUDE
Tuckahoe 1972–1978

THE AFFAIR
Montauk 2014–present

SLEEPY HOLLOW
Sleepy Hollow 2013–2017

NIAGARA FALLS

UPSTATE

FOX RIDGE

WELLSVILLE

PEEKSKILL

HASTINGS-ON-HUDSON

TUCKAHOE

BEACON

SLEEPY HOLLOW

GRANDVIEW

LONG ISLAND

MONTAUK

NEW YORK CITY

THE HAMPTONS

PEOPLE OF EARTH
Beacon 2016–2017

GHOST WHISPERER
Grandview 2005–2010

WITCHES OF EAST END
Northampton 2013–2014

ROOM 104 Long Island 2017–present

EVERYBODY LOVES RAYMOND
Lynnbrook, Long Island 1996–2005

ROYAL PAINS Southampton 2009–2016

REVENGE
The Hamptons 2011–2015

NEW YORK CITY

THE GOLDBERGS 1949–1957

THE DANNY THOMAS SHOW 1953–1964

PRIVATE SECRETARY 1953–1957

NAKED CITY 1958–1959 & 1960–1963

CAR 54, WHERE ARE YOU? 1961–1963

GREEN ACRES 1965–1971

THAT GIRL 1966–1971

BROOKLYN

THE PATTY DUKE SHOW 1963–1966

THE COSBY SHOW 1984–1992

LIVING SINGLE 1993–1998

EVERYBODY HATES CHRIS 2005–2009

IN TREATMENT 2008–2010

BROOKLYN NINE-NINE 2013–present

HUSTLE 2013

SHE'S GOTTA HAVE IT 2017–present

THE LAST O.G. 2018–present

CHAMPIONS Brooklyn 2018
There's no better place for a workout than Champions gym, one of the few spots in the borough not ruined by gentrification. Or modern equipment.

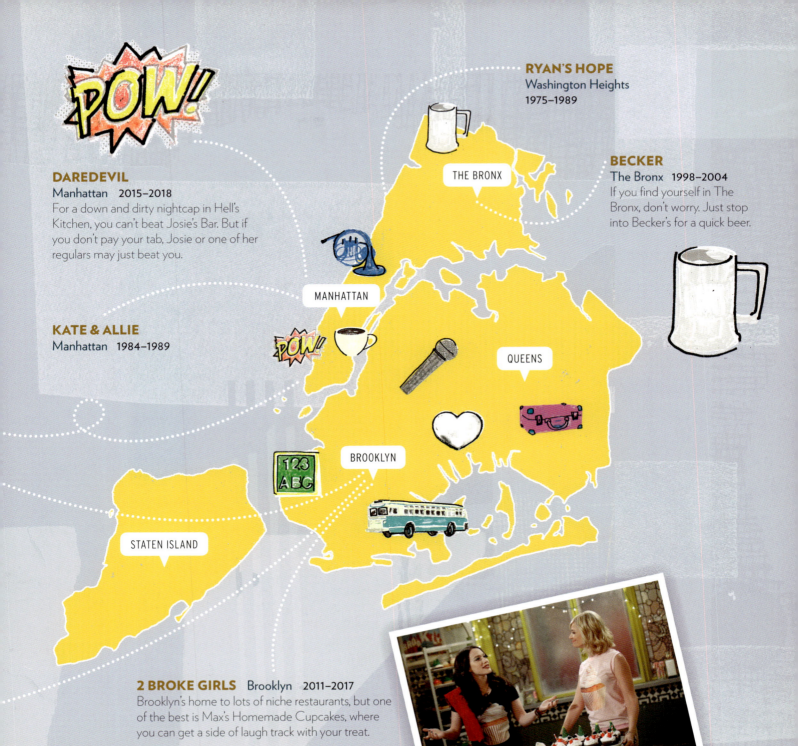

RYAN'S HOPE
Washington Heights
1975–1989

DAREDEVIL
Manhattan   2015–2018
For a down and dirty nightcap in Hell's Kitchen, you can't beat Josie's Bar. But if you don't pay your tab, Josie or one of her regulars may just beat you.

BECKER
The Bronx   1998–2004
If you find yourself in The Bronx, don't worry. Just stop into Becker's for a quick beer.

KATE & ALLIE
Manhattan   1984–1989

THE BRONX

MANHATTAN

QUEENS

BROOKLYN

STATEN ISLAND

2 BROKE GIRLS   Brooklyn   2011–2017
Brooklyn's home to lots of niche restaurants, but one of the best is Max's Homemade Cupcakes, where you can get a side of laugh track with your treat.

NEW YORK CITY

THE DICK VAN DYKE SHOW
1961–1966

FAMILY AFFAIR 1966–1971; revival 2002–2003

THE ODD COUPLE 1970–1975; revival 2015–2017

WELCOME BACK, KOTTER 1975–1979

THE AMAZING SPIDER-MAN 1977–1979

FISH 1977–1978

TAXI 1978–1982

MRS. COLUMBO 1979–1980

BOSOM BUDDIES 1980–1982

CHECKING IN 1981

FAME 1982–1987

WE GOT IT MADE 1983–1984

THE EQUALIZER 1985–1989

MY TWO DADS 1987–1990

DEAR JOHN 1988–1992

DREAM ON 1990–1996

MAD ABOUT YOU 1992–1999

SPIN CITY 1996–2002

CAROLINE IN THE CITY 1995–1999

CUPID 1998–1999; revival 2009

FELICITY 1998–2002

LAW & ORDER: SVU
1999–present

**DON'T TRUST THE B----
IN APARTMENT 23**
2012–2013

YOUNGER
2015–present

THE BRONX

MANHATTAN

QUEENS

POW!

BROOKLYN

123
ABC

STATEN ISLAND

RHODA 1974–1978
Whether designed by Simon Doonan, Tiffany, or Windows by Rhoda, you'll get verklempt at the beautifully designed department store window displays that line Fifth Avenue during the holidays.

THE HONEYMOONERS Brooklyn 1955–1956
New York's transit system is the best in the world. Use the trains to get places quickly, but for a great sightseeing tour, the extensive bus lines will take you to the moon!

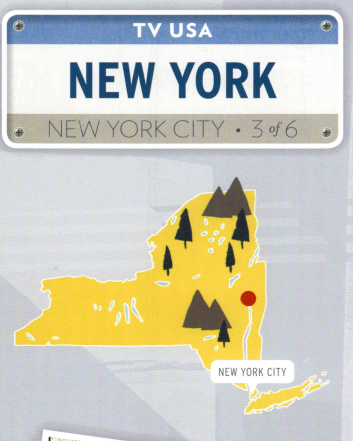

NEW YORK CITY

CAGNEY & LACEY 1982–1988

NIGHT COURT 1984–1992

HEAD OF THE CLASS 1986–1991

HERMAN'S HEAD 1991–1994

NYPD BLUE 1993–2005

NEWSRADIO 1995–1999

THE CRITIC 1994–2001

VERONICA'S CLOSET 1997–2000

FUTURAMA 1999–2013

NOW AND AGAIN 1999–2000

TIME OF YOUR LIFE 1999–2000

ZOE, DUNCAN, JACK & JANE 1999–2000

MANHATTAN

BARNEY MILLER 1975–1982

DIFF'RENT STROKES 1978–1986

30 ROCK 2006–2013

BEAUTY AND THE BEAST 2012–2016

ANGIE TRIBECA 2016–present

SEX AND THE CITY 1998–2004
Greenwich Village's own Magnolia Bakery is the place to go for a quick treat. There are ore than just cupcakes—be sure to check out the incredible banana pudding!

LUKE CAGE
Harlem 2016–2018
Music lovers flock to Harlem's Paradise, a mainstay that has offered musicians of all genres the opportunity to play for the community for generations.

THE JEFFERSONS
Manhattan 1975–1985
For the best dry cleaning in Manhattan, you can't beat Jefferson Cleaners. Located in multiple locations around Manhattan, the spot on the East Side is considered the most deluxe.

NEW AMSTERDAM
2018–present

JESSICA JONES
2015–present

LIPSTICK JUNGLE
2008–2009

LOVE, SIDNEY
1981–1983

SEINFELD
1989–1998

LAW & ORDER
1990–2010

DIFFICULT PEOPLE
2015–2017

THE BRONX

MANHATTAN

POW

QUEENS

BROOKLYN

123 ABC

STATEN ISLAND

NEW YORK CITY

ED 2000–2004

LAW & ORDER: CRIMINAL INTENT 2001–2011

CSI: NEW YORK 2004–2013

RESCUE ME 2004–2011

AMERICAN DRAGON: JAKE LONG 2005–2007

LAW & ORDER: TRIAL BY JURY 2005–2006

HEROES 2006–2010

UGLY BETTY 2006–2010

THE BLACK DONNELYS 2007

DAMAGES 2007–2012

THE FLIGHT OF THE CONCHORDS 2007–2009

GOSSIP GIRL 2007–2012

MAD MEN 2007–2015

THE NAKED BROTHERS BAND 2007–2009

WIZARDS OF WAVERLY PLACE 2007–2012

THE CITY 2008–2010

LIFE ON MARS 2008–2009

TRUE JACKSON: VP 2008–2011

HOW I MET YOUR MOTHER 2005–2014

**THE SUITE LIFE
OF ZACK & CODY**
2005–2008

THE DEFENDERS 2017
Locals love ordering Chinese
takeout from The Royal
Dragon. Try the specials!

THE BRONX

MANHATTAN

QUEENS

BROOKLYN

STATEN ISLAND

FRIENDS
1994–2004

NURSE JACKIE
2009–2015

**THE LIFE AND
TIMES OF TIM**
2008–2012

KOJAK
2005

IRON FIST 2017–2018
New York can be a tough place. But The
Chikara Dojo has been training folks of
all ages the art of self-defense for years.

GROUNDED FOR LIFE
Staten Island   2001–2005

NEW YORK CITY

THE MARVELOUS MRS. MAISEL 2017–present

RULES OF ENGAGEMENT 2007–2013

ARCHER 2009–present

CASTLE 2009–2016

BLUE BLOODS 2010–present

HOW TO MAKE IT IN AMERICA 2010–2011

RIZZOLI AND ISLES 2010–2016

FRANKLIN AND BASH 2011–2014

JESSIE 2011–2015

SUITS 2011–present

BABY DADDY 2012–2017

GIRLS 2012–2017

HIGH MAINTENANCE 2012–present

MEN AT WORK 2012–2014

THE MINDY PROJECT 2012–2017

QUEENS

ALL IN THE FAMILY 1971–1979

704 HAUSER 1994

THE KING OF QUEENS 1998–2007

SWEETBITTER
2018–present

THE BRONX

ARCHIE BUNKER'S PLACE
Queens   1979–1983
For an authentic Queens bar experience, check out this local watering hole whose namesake proprietor has as many opinions as he does beers on tap.

MANHATTAN

QUEENS

CRASHING
2017–present

BROOKLYN

STATEN ISLAND

BEING MARY JANE
2013–present

WORKING GIRL
Staten Island   1990

THE BLACKLIST
2013–present

SESAME STREET   1969–present
You'll find everything you need for comfort and care at Hooper's Grocery store, located on Sesame Street.

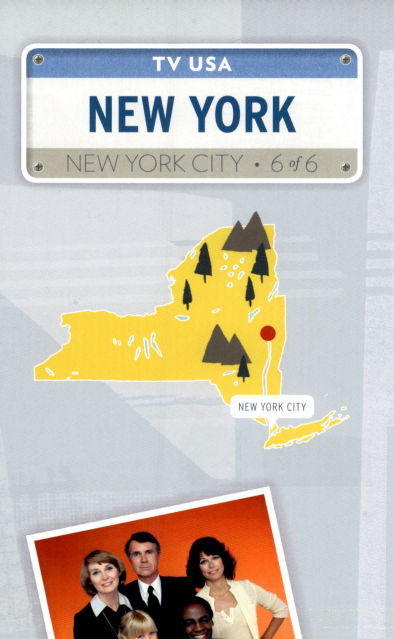

NEW YORK CITY

BENSON 1979–1986

ELEMENTARY 2012–present

GIRL MEETS WORLD 2014–2017

THE KNICK 2014–2015

MOZART IN THE JUNGLE 2014–2018

POWER 2014–present

BLINDSPOT 2015–present

EMPIRE 2015–present

MASTER OF NONE 2015–present

MR. ROBOT 2015–present

ODD MOM OUT 2015–2017

SNEAKY PETE 2015–present

SEARCH PARTY 2016–present

SHADES OF BLUE 2016–2018

SHADOWHUNTERS 2016–present

VINYL 2016

THE DEUCE 2017–present

FOR THE PEOPLE 2018–present

FRIENDS FROM COLLEGE 2017–present

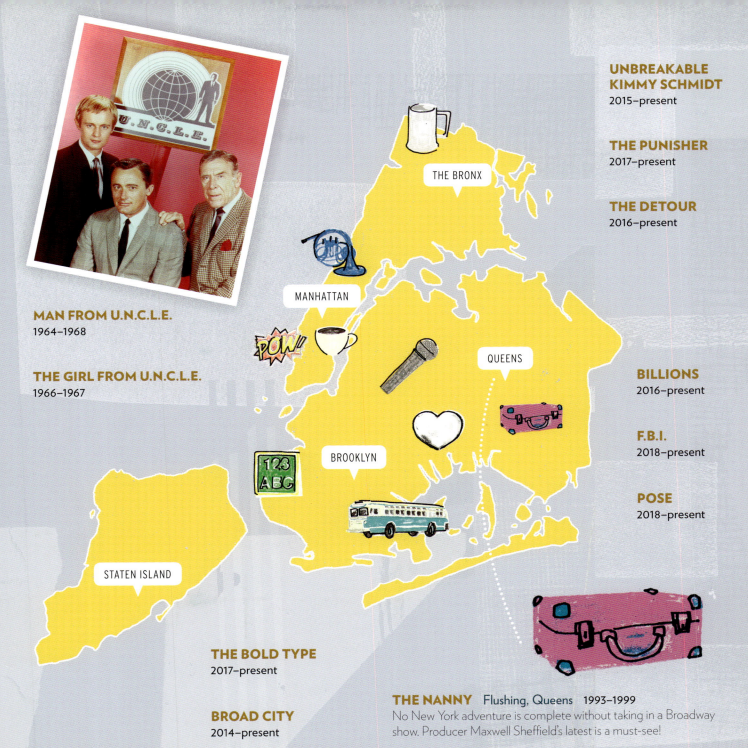

UNBREAKABLE
KIMMY SCHMIDT
2015–present

THE PUNISHER
2017–present

THE DETOUR
2016–present

THE BRONX

MANHATTAN

MAN FROM U.N.C.L.E.
1964–1968

THE GIRL FROM U.N.C.L.E.
1966–1967

QUEENS

BILLIONS
2016–present

F.B.I.
2018–present

BROOKLYN

POSE
2018–present

STATEN ISLAND

THE BOLD TYPE
2017–present

BROAD CITY
2014–present

THE NANNY   Flushing, Queens   1993–1999
No New York adventure is complete without taking in a Broadway show. Producer Maxwell Sheffield's latest is a must-see!

TV USA

NORTH CAROLINA

Sit back, relax, and kick up your tar heels for a great time in North Carolina. If the majesty of The Great Smoky Mountains National Park doesn't blow you away, perhaps the splendor of the Biltmore Estate will do the trick. If not, just keep repeating the name of the Marbles Kids Museum over and over as you tour beautiful downtown Raleigh and that'll put a smile on your face.

THE ANDY GRIFFITH SHOW
Mayberry (fic.) 1960–1968

MAYBERRY, RFD
Mayberry (fic.) 2015–2017
If you find yourself stranded in a small town, you could do a lot worse than Mayberry, the "Garden City of the State." While your car gets fixed at Wally's Filling Station, get a haircut at Floyd's Barber Shop and a bite to eat at The Bluebird Diner. If you're looking for more, stop by the Greater Mayberry Historical Society and Tourist Bureau.

AMERICAN HORROR STORY
Roanoke Island   2011–present
Take a hike in the dense woods surrounding Roanoke! Site of the century-old mystery surrounding the famed "Lost Colony," locals and visitors still report seeing strange things, in addition to beautiful sunsets and wildlife.

ROANOKE

SHELLBY

CHARLOTTE

EASTBOUND & DOWN   Shelby   2009–2013
Be sure to pop in to Ashley Schaeffer BMW on your way through Shelby to catch a pitch from hometown hero, baseball's Kenny Powers!

THE CARMICHAEL SHOW
Charlotte   2015–2017

ONE TREE HILL
Tree Hill (fic.)   2003–2012

TV USA

NORTH DAKOTA

Sometimes called the least-visited state in America, tourists and natives alike still find peace in the Roughrider State. Though television's Lawrence Welk, a native of North Dakota, may have traded his walks through Theodore Roosevelt National Park for bubble-filled evenings in Manhattan, you'll certainly find something good to do. Or at least something good on television.

BLOOD AND OIL
Rock Springs (fic.) 2015
Despite the surge in money surrounding the oil fields in and around Rock Springs, there seems to be only one bar. This one, owned by Jules Jackman, can offer you some "bread" with your beers.

TV USA

OHIO

GLEE Lima 2009–2015
If you have an appetite for Italian food with a side of showtunes, make a reservation at Breadstix where you'll find your fill of pasta and covers of today's popular music.

WKRP IN CINCINNATI
Cincinnati 1978–1982
Cincinnati has a wide variety of cultural events and entertainment. For the most up-to-the-minute information, locals tune in to WKRP, where local newsman Les Nessman fills them in on everything from Turkey Drops to traffic.

MARY HARTMAN, MARY HARTMAN
Fernwood (fic.) 1976–1977

FERNWOOD TONIGHT Fernwood (fic.) 1977

HOMEFRONT Riverrun (fic.) 1991–1993

HOPE AND FAITH Glen Falls (fic.) 2003–2006

GREEK 2007–2011

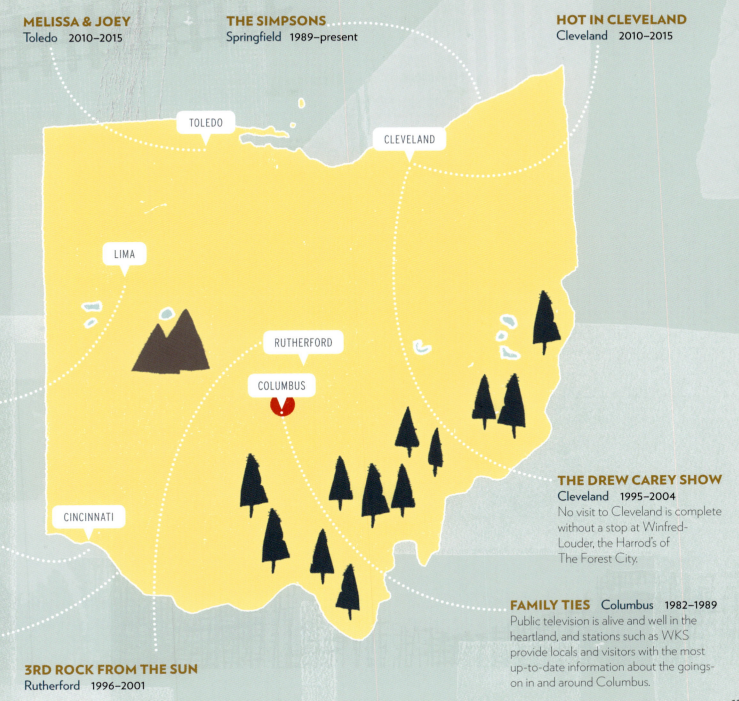

MELISSA & JOEY
Toledo   2010–2015

THE SIMPSONS
Springfield   1989–present

HOT IN CLEVELAND
Cleveland   2010–2015

TOLEDO

CLEVELAND

LIMA

RUTHERFORD

COLUMBUS

CINCINNATI

THE DREW CAREY SHOW
Cleveland   1995–2004
No visit to Cleveland is complete
without a stop at Winfred-
Louder, the Harrod's of
The Forest City.

FAMILY TIES   Columbus   1982–1989
Public television is alive and well in the
heartland, and stations such as WKS
provide locals and visitors with the most
up-to-date information about the goings-
on in and around Columbus.

3RD ROCK FROM THE SUN
Rutherford   1996–2001

127

Volunteer tourism is a wonderful way for travelers of all ages to give back to communities while exploring different locales. Be sure to wear the right outfit for the job, though—a pair of stretchy comfortable pants is always a good bet. These are some of the locations where you can lend a hand:

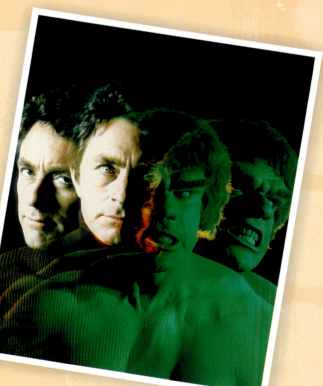

1. "Final Round": Wilmington, DE

2. "The Beast Within": San Diego, CA

3. "Mystery Man" Parts 1 and 2: Santa Fe, NM

4. "Escape from Los Santos": Lost Santos, AZ

5. "Homecoming": CO

6. "Slaves": LA

7. "Interview with the Hulk": Chicago, IL, and Atlanta, GA

8. "The First" Parts 1 and 2: Vissaria (fic.)

9. "King of the Beach": Santa Monica, CA

10. "Equinox": ME

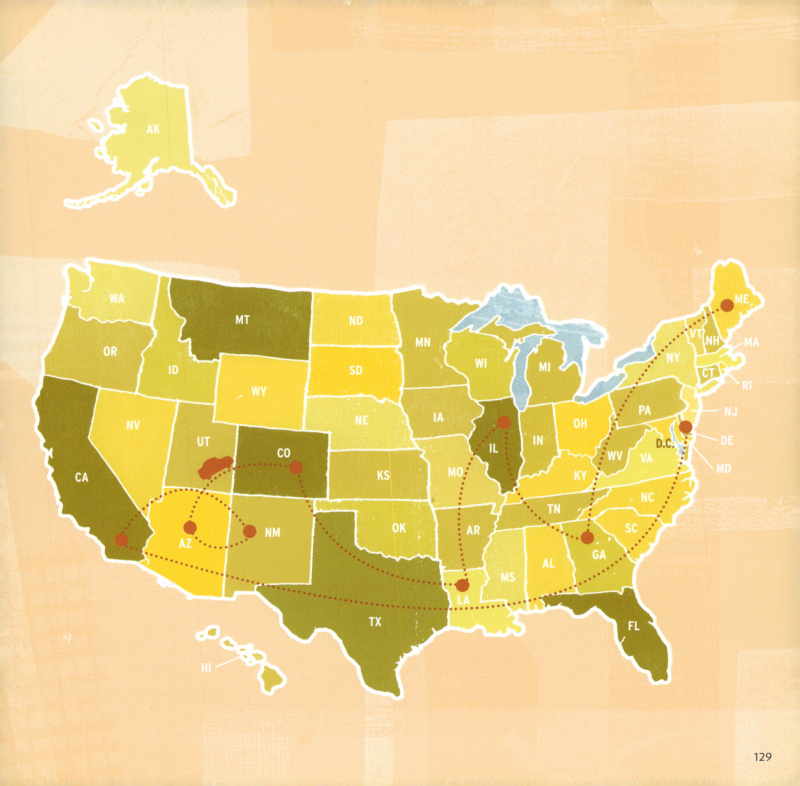

OKLAHOMA

OK, OK, I get it. You think you'd sooner watch the Travel Channel than travel to The Sooner State, but where else, other than your television, could you see bison roaming the prairies, encounter members of more than sixty-five Native American tribes, and dance along to a square dance? Only in Oklahoma. OK?

AGENT CARTER
Broxton   2015–2016
When driving through Broxton, stop by the home where famed actress Whitney Frost grew up!

INTO THE BADLANDS
2015–present

MR. ED
1961–1966

MILFAY

OKLAHOMA CITY

BROXTON

SAVING GRACE
Oklahoma City   2007–2010

CARNIVÀLE
Milfay   2003–2005

GRACE UNDER FIRE
Oklahoma City   1993–1998

131

PORTLAND

PORTLANDIA Portland 2011–2018
Candace and Toni, the proprietors of
Women and Women First, Portland's
premiere femimist bookstore, may seem off-
putting but don't worry, they are.

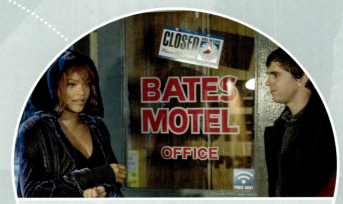

BATES MOTEL
White Pine Bay (fic.)   2013–2017
White Pine Bay offers beautiful seaside views, perfect for a long weekend. Check out the Bates Motel, where you'll find a welcoming staff and newly renovated bathrooms.

BEST FRIENDS WHENEVER
Portland   2015–2016

GRIMM
Portland   2011–2017

EUREKA
Eureka (fic.)   2006–2012

THE SIMPSONS
Springfield   1989–present

LIFE SENTENCE
Nashville (fic.)   2018

TV USA
PENNSYLVANIA

SULLIVAN & SON Pittsburgh 2012–2014
There's nothing quite like a no-frills bar to relax after a hard day's work (or travel). Be sure to stop by Sullivan & Son, where the locals go for a cold beer and good conversation.

BANSHEE
Banshee 2013–2016

QUEER AS FOLK
Pittsburgh 2000–2005
After a long night at the clubs, there's no better place to relax, and carbo-load, than The Liberty Diner, located on Liberty Street. If you're in need (or even if you're not), head waitress and mom-to-everyone Debbie will offer breakfast 24/7, with a side of wisdom.

BANSHEE

PITTSBURGH

PITTSBURGH

MY SO-CALLED LIFE 1994–1995

HOPE AND GLORIA 1995–1996

REMEMBER WENN 1996–1998

THIS IS US 2016–present

THE GOLDBERGS
Jenkintown 2013–present
Do your shopping at the Ottoman Empire and pick up a shelving unit for your videotapes.

STAR TREK: ENTERPRISE
Carbon Creek 2001–2005
Stop by Carbon Creek, a simple mining town in Pennsylvania, where you can tour the mines and hear locals talk about how it was there, not Boseman, Montana, or Roswell, New Mexico, that humans' first contact with aliens occurred!

CARBON CREEK

MORRISTOWN

SCRANTON

HEMLOCK GROVE

JENKINTOWN

LEVITTOWN

BROCKMIRE
Morristown
2017–present

HEMLOCK GROVE
Hemlock Grove
2013–2015

MISTER ROGERS' NEIGHBORHOOD
1968–2001

THE OFFICE Scranton 2005–2013
Located within driving distance of the Scranton branch of Dunder Mifflin, Schrute Farm, is the perfect bed and breakfast destination if you're in the mood to spend the weekend inside PA. That's what she said.

ALL MY CHILDREN Pine Valley (fic.) 1970–2011

LOVING Corinth (fic.) 1983–1995

MR. BELVEDERE Beaver Falls (fic.) 1985–1990

PRETTY LITTLE LIARS Rosewood (fic.) 2010–2017

RAVENSWOOD Ravenswood (fic.) 2013–2014

RISE
Levittown 2018

TV USA

PENNSYLVANIA

PHILADELPHIA

ONE LIFE TO LIVE 1968–2012; revival 2013

ANGIE 1979–1980

BROTHERS 1984–1989

THIRTYSOMETHING 1987–1991

BOY MEETS WORLD 1993–2000

STRONG MEDICINE 2000–2006

HOW TO GET AWAY WITH MURDER
2014–present

12 MONKEYS 2015–present

PHILADELPHIA

BOY MEETS WORLD 1993–2000

AMEN 1986–1991
If you find yourself in the City of Brotherly Love on a Sunday, stop by Deacon Frye's First Community Church for a rousing service.

IT'S ALWAYS SUNNY IN PHILADELPHIA 2005–present
There are many fantastic watering holes in South Philly, but none will make you feel more uncomfortable, or smarter, on a sunny day than Paddy's Pub.

BROTHERHOOD
Providence   2006–2008

FAMILY GUY
Quahog (fic.)   1999–present
You'll have a great time grabbing a beer or cocktail at The Drunken Clam. Just like the time you cut away to a similar pop culture reference that treads the line between humor and vulgarity.

PROVIDENCE

NEWPORT

PROVIDENCE
Providence 1999–2002

The smallest state in the union may not be an island, but all roads lead to fun in Little Rhody! Whether you're chowing on chowder in Pawtucket or sipping cocktails in Newport, there are lots of local flavors, or, in this case, *flavahs*, to enjoy.

ANOTHER PERIOD
Newport 2015–present

TV USA
SOUTH CAROLINA

Whether you're a Daughter of the American Revolution slowly walking through Charleston or a brother of a college fraternity quickly drinking your way through Myrtle Beach, South Carolina has something for you. The Palmetto State's beautiful beaches, historic sites, and delicious food make any trip to this Southern state one to remember.

VICE PRINCIPALS
2016–2017
South Carolina may first in beautiful shoreline and historic sights, but it sadly ranks last in education. Schools like North Jackson High School, where students come second, may be the cause.

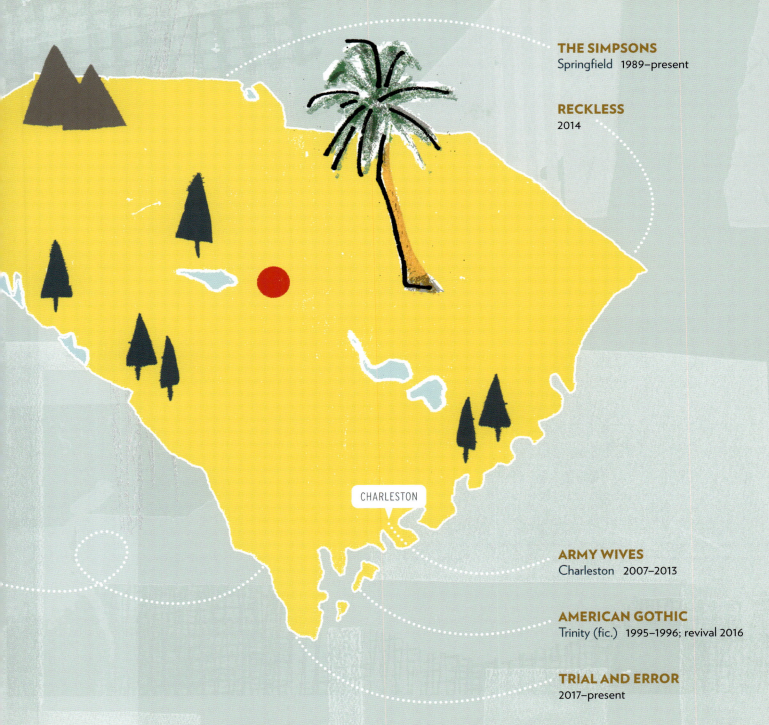

THE SIMPSONS
Springfield 1989–present

RECKLESS
2014

ARMY WIVES
Charleston 2007–2013

AMERICAN GOTHIC
Trinity (fic.) 1995–1996; revival 2016

TRIAL AND ERROR
2017–present

CHARLESTON

TV USA
SOUTH DAKOTA

THE SIMPSONS
Springfield   1989–present

If television had been invented before 1941, the faces of Mount Rushmore could have been Oprah Winfrey, Linda Bloodworth-Thompson, Susan Harris, and Shonda Rhimes. But it wasn't, so we have the presidents, instead. Which is nice, too.

DEADWOOD
Deadwood   2004–2006
If you're in the mood for some international flavors, check into the Chez Ami for an evening (or afternoon) delight.

DEADWOOD

WAREHOUSE 13
2009–2014
If there's one thing you should stop to see in South Dakota it's Mount Rushmore. If there's one thing you shouldn't stop at, it's an unmarked warehouse in the middle of nowhere. Just keep driving. Nothing to see there. Nothing at all.

TV USA

TENNESSEE

THE SIMPSONS
Springfield   1989–present

HELLCATS
Memphis   2010–2011

GREENLEAF
Memphis   2016–present
Stop by Calvary Fellowship any Sunday for a inspiring sermon by Bishop James Greenleaf.

You'll want to volunteer to visit Tennessee any time of year to enjoy any number of musical treasures. Whether it's taking in a show at the famed Grand Ole Opry, spending the day at Dollywood in Pigeon Forge, or visiting Graceland in Memphis, a visit to Tennessee will fuel your soul with more songs than you can add to your playlist.

MEMPHIS

NASHVILLE
Nashville 2012–2018

NASHVILLE

DELTA
1992–1993

MEMPHIS BEAT
Memphis 2010–2011

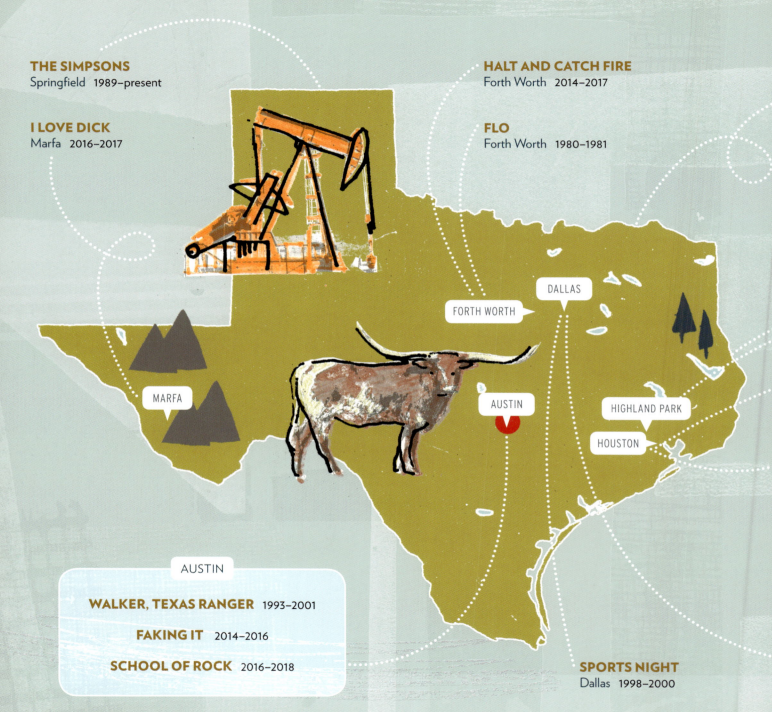

THE SIMPSONS
Springfield 1989–present

I LOVE DICK
Marfa 2016–2017

HALT AND CATCH FIRE
Forth Worth 2014–2017

FLO
Forth Worth 1980–1981

DALLAS

FORTH WORTH

MARFA

AUSTIN

HIGHLAND PARK

HOUSTON

AUSTIN

WALKER, TEXAS RANGER 1993–2001

FAKING IT 2014–2016

SCHOOL OF ROCK 2016–2018

SPORTS NIGHT
Dallas 1998–2000

TEXAS

THE LONE RANGER 1949–1957

TEXAS 1980–1982

SORDID LIVES: THE SERIES 2008

THE CLIENT LIST 2012–2013

THE SON 2017–present

YOUNG SHELDON 2017–present

BEAVIS & BUTT-HEAD
Highland (fic.) 1993–1997; revival 2011

GCB
Highland Park 2012

LONE STAR
Houston 2010

REBA
Houston 2001–2007

DALLAS
Dallas 1978–1991; revival 2012–2014

KING OF THE HILL Arlen (fic.) 1997–2010

**THE ADVENTURES OF
JIMMY NEUTRON BOY GENIUS**
Retroville (fic.) 2002–2006

FRIDAY NIGHT LIGHTS Dillon (fic.) 2006–present

HAP AND LEONARD La Borde (fic.) 2016–2018

PREACHER Annville (fic.) 2016–present

MIDNIGHT, TEXAS Midnight (fic.) 2017–present

UTAH

BIG LOVE
Salt Lake City   2006–2011
Buck the big-box chains and do all of your hardware shopping at Home Plus. Owned and operated by Utah's own Bill Henrickson and his sizable family, you'll find just what you need for everything from simple home repairs to major renovations.

AIRWOLF
1984–1987

ANDI MACK
2017–present

THE BOYS OF TWILIGHT
Twilight (fic.)   1992

SALT LAKE CITY

TV USA
VERMONT

Millions of people vacation in The Green Mountain State every year. Whether you're into fishing, skiing, hiking, or just getting away from it all, it offers something for every outdoorsy person. And for those indoorsy sorts, it offers a full selection of bingeable series on cable and streaming services!

NEWHART 1982–1990
Vermont is home to hundreds of quaint hotels and bed and breakfasts, but check in to the Stratford Inn, where proprietor and author Dick Loudon and his wife, Joanna, will provide you with such a good night's sleep you'll feel like you've been dreaming for eight years.

THE SIMPSONS
Springfield   1989–present

THE NEW LASSIE
Hudson Falls (fic.)   1989–1992

THREE MOONS OVER MILFORD
Milford (fic.)   2006

TV USA

VIRGINIA

QUANTICO Quantico 2015–2018
If you're visiting Washington, D.C., it's just a
short trip to Virginia where you can take a
tour of the training facility of the FBI.

HANNIBAL
2013–2015

A DIFFERENT WORLD Hillman College (fic.) 1987–1993

THE SIMPSONS Springfield 1989–present

AMERICAN DAD! Langley Falls (fic.) 2005–present

THE VAMPIRE DIARIES Mystic Falls (fic.) 2009–2017

CRIMINAL MINDS
Quantico 2005–present

CRIMINAL MINDS: SUSPECT BEHAVIOR
Quantico 2011

HOMELAND
Langley 2011–present
And while visiting the FBI, check out the CIA's training facility!

QUANTICO

LANGLEY

VIRGINIA BEACH

FINDING CARTER
Fairfax (fic.) 2014–2015

SEAL TEAM
Virginia Beach 2017–present

THE WALTONS
Jefferson County (fic.) 1972–1981

SEATTLE

TWIN PEAKS Twin Peaks (fic.)
1990–1991, Special 1992; revival 2017

HEY ARNOLD! Hillwood (fic.) 1996–2004

THE SECRET CIRCLE Chance Harbor (fic.) 2011–2012

SEATTLE

CHARLES IN CHARGE 1984–1990

DEAD LIKE ME 2003–2004

ROMEO! 2003–2006

LIFE AS WE KNOW IT 2004–2005

GREY'S ANATOMY 2005–present

KYLE XY 2006–2009

EXES AND OHS 2007; 2011

iCARLY 2007–2012

ARE WE THERE YET? 2010–2013

THE KILLING 2011–2014

RICK AND MORTY 2013–present

iZOMBIE 2015–present

STATION 19 2018–present

FRASIER Seattle 1993–2004
Bucking the chain-coffee-shop trend born in Seattle, Café Nervosa's sole location is famous not only for its delicious brew, but for hosting many of radio station KACL's on-air personalities.

TV USA

WEST VIRGINIA

The historic and scenic Mountain State is so independent it not only seceded from the Union, it seceded from Virginia! But even after all that seceding, it has still succeeded in remaining one of the most beautiful and hard-working states in the nation. And after all that nature watching and hard work, what better way to unwind than watching everything on your DVR!

HAWKINS
1973–1974
If you find yourself in trouble in West Virginia (and let's face it, you will), we suggest you contact lawyer Billy Jim Hawkins to get you out of it.

THE SIMPSONS
Springfield 1989–present

HARPER'S FERRY

THE AMERICANS
Harper's Ferry 1961
There are few places in America with as much historical significance as Harper's Ferry, West Virginia. Here you'll find the spot where abolitionist John Brown led a raid, and where "Stonewall" Jackson led the Confederates in the Civil War's Battle of Harpers Ferry, cleaving not only the nation, but the Canfield family as well.

TV USA

TV ROAD TRIP

THE TWILIGHT ZONE • 1959–1964

In a country filled with as many mind-blowing locations as the United States, you'll discover that no place is ever exactly what you think it is. For experiences that are rarely just black-and-white, follow the signpost up ahead. Here are just a few places to check out:

1. "Still Valley": VA

2. "To Serve Man": NY

3. "Jess-Belle": Blue Ridge Mountains

4. "Valley of the Shadow": NM

5. "An Occurrence at Owl Creek Bridge": AL

6. "A Game of Pool": Chicago, IL

7. "The Monsters Are Due on Maple Street": Maple Street, US

8. "The Hitch-Hiker": PA

9. "Nightmare at 20,000 Feet": In the air over the US

10. "The Masks": New Orleans, LA

TV USA

WISCONSIN

THE SIMPSONS
Springfield   1989–present

PICKET FENCES
Rome   1992–1996

THE BRIGHTER DAY
New Hope   1954–1962

THAT 70S SHOW
Point Place (fic.)   1998–2006
If you're still using a camera with film, you might want to stop by the Foto Hut, where you can get film developed in a few days.

LAVERNE & SHIRLEY
Milwaukee   1976–1983
Take a tour of the famous Schott's Brewing Factory. You'll get a free sip of beer and sometimes a free glove, too!

LIV AND MADDIE
Stevens Point   2013–2017

STEP BY STEP
Port Washington   1991–1998

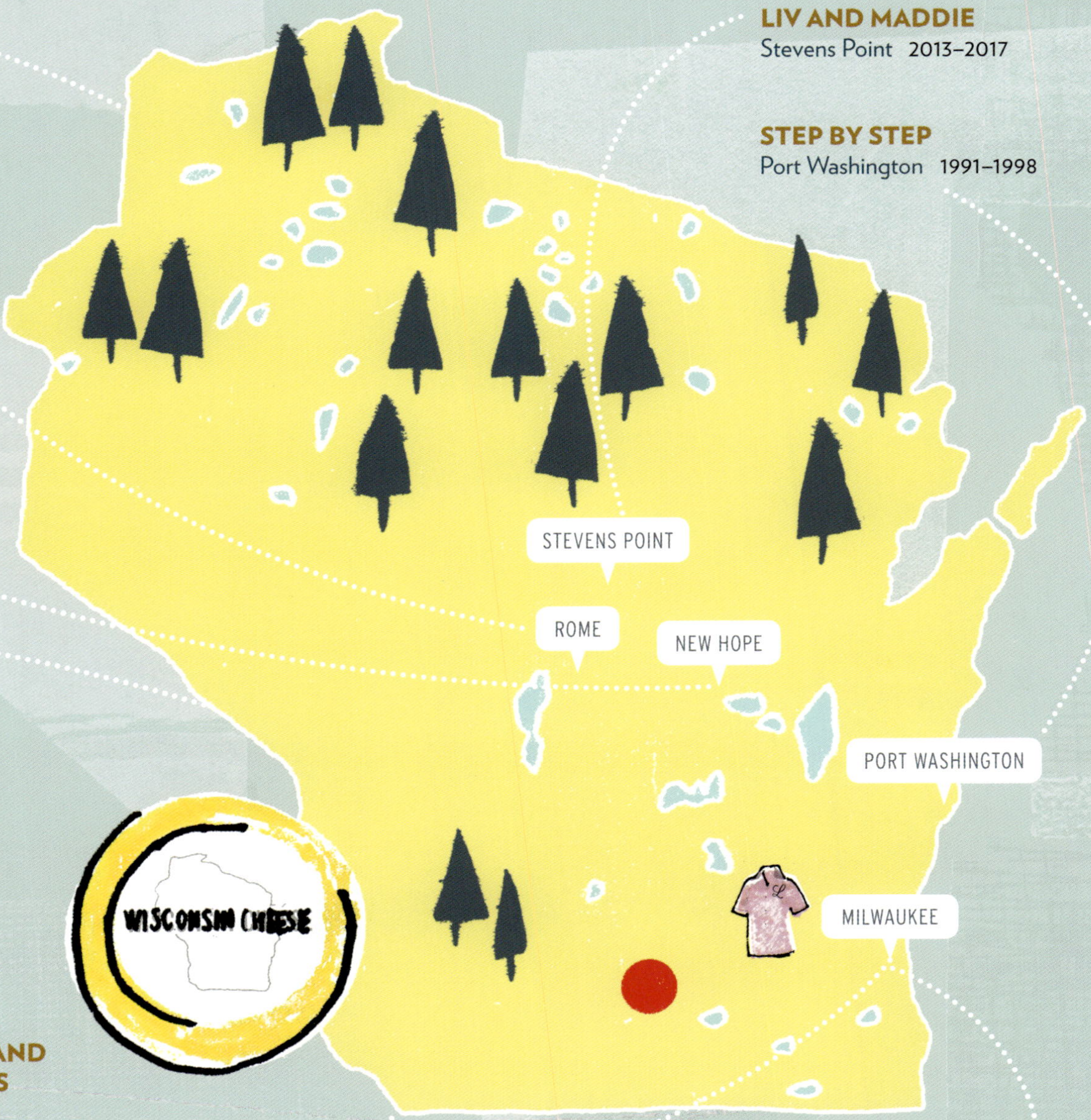

STEVENS POINT

ROME

NEW HOPE

PORT WASHINGTON

WISCONSIN CHEESE

MILWAUKEE

THE YOUNG AND
THE RESTLESS
Genoa City (fic.)
1973–present

HAPPY DAYS
Milwaukee   1974–1984

WYOMING

Why not? The Equality State has equal opportunities for any network to succeed, though the natural wonders of The Devils Tower National Monument give syndicated programs about angels a run for their money. Though you'll encounter bears in Yellowstone National Park, they'll be quite different than those found in Jellystone (especially when it comes to pic-a-nic baskets).

LONGMIRE
Absaroka County (fic.) 2012–2017

MEDICINE BOW

THE VIRGINIAN

Medicine Bow 1962–1971

For a rootin' tootin' good time, stop by the Shiloh Ranch,
where you can ride horses, bale hay, and sharpshoot.

TV USA

WASHINGTON, DC

THE AMERICANS
2013–2018

WOMEN OF THE HOUSE 1995
Be sure to stop by the House of Representatives to say hi to, or lodge a complaint with, your local congressperson. Remember, they work for you!

CAPITOL 1982–1987

SMART GUY 1997–1999

THE SECRET DIARY OF DESMOND PFEFFER
1998

BONES 2005–2017

COVERT AFFAIRS 2010–2014

1600 PENN 2012–2013

SCANDAL 2012–2018

VEEP 2012–present

MADAM SECRETARY 2014–present

CSI: CYBER 2015–2016

K.C. UNDERCOVER 2015–2018

DESIGNATED SURVIVOR 2016–2018

THE GIRLFRIEND EXPERIENCE 2016–present

THE WEST WING 1999–2006
No stop to Washington, D.C., is complete without a tour of The White House. Regardless of the administration, and despite its troublesome construction, the building itself is a testament to the strength of the country.

MURPHY BROWN 1988–1998; revival 2018
Stop by Phil's for traditional pub grub served up with a side of Washington insider gossip and politics.

HOUSE OF CARDS 2013–2018
For the best barbecue in all of Washington, D.C., you must stop by Freddy's. Though it looks like a hole-in-the-wall, its clientele includes everyone from blue collar guys to political powerhouses. Remember to ask for extra napkins.

WONDER WOMAN 1975–1979
The nation's capital is filled with man-made wonders, but they pale in comparison to Wonder Woman, who you may find saving someone from a killer robot or in and around The Mall.

227 1985–1990

SEARCH FOR TOMORROW
Salem (fic.) 1951–1986

ADVENTURES OF SUPERMAN Metropolis (fic.)
1952–1958

HAZEL 1961–1966

THE DOCTORS Madison (fic.) 1963–1982

THE ADDAMS FAMILY 1964–1966

PEYTON PLACE Peyton Place (fic.) 1964–1969

BATMAN Gotham City 1966–1968

THE MOTHERS-IN-LAW 1967–1969

THE SECRETS OF ISIS 1975–1977

I'M A BIG GIRL NOW 1980–1981

HILL STREET BLUES 1981–1987

SILVER SPOONS 1982–1987

THE LAW & HARRY MCGRAW 1987–1988

WISEGUY 1987–1990

MISSION HILL
Mission Hill (fic.) 1999–2002

OZ
Emerald City (fic.) 1997–2003

LOIS & CLARK
Metropolis (fic.) 1993–1997

PASSIONS
Harmony (fic.) 1999–2007

THE SUITE LIFE ON DECK
SS *Tipton* (fic.) 2008–2011

DR. KATZ, PROFESSIONAL THERAPIST
1995–2002

ALLEN GREGORY
2011

BLACK DYNAMITE
2012–2015

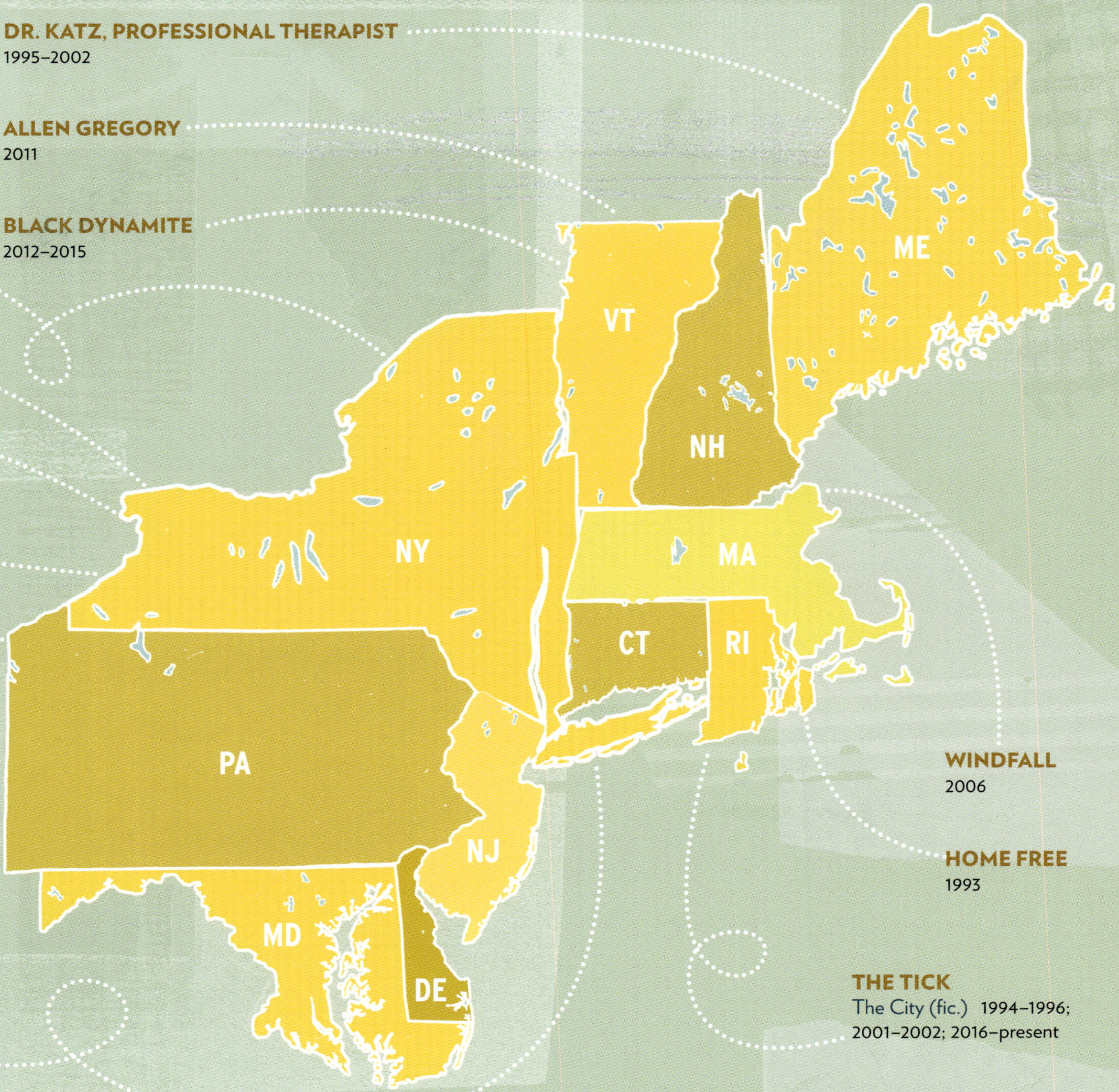

WINDFALL
2006

HOME FREE
1993

THE TICK
The City (fic.) 1994–1996;
2001–2002; 2016–present

ME

VT

NH

NY

MA

CT   RI

PA

NJ

MD

DE

POPULAR 1999–2001

HOME MOVIES 1999–2004

GIDEON'S CROSSING 2000–2001

UNFABULOUS 2004–2007

THE NINE 2006–2007

TELL ME YOU LOVE ME 2007

HARPER'S ISLAND Harper's Island 2009

BLACK DYNAMITE 2012–2015

GO ON 2012–2013

THE NEWSROOM 2012–2014

ORPHAN BLACK 2013–2017

THE OA 2016–present

DEAR WHITE PEOPLE 2017–present

MARY KILLS PEOPLE 2017–present

POWERLESS Charm City (fic.) 2017

RIVERDALE Riverdale (fic.) 2017–present

ALEX, INC. 2018

SIREN Bristol Cove (fic.) 2018–present

PUSHING DAISIES 2007–2009

THE LONE GUNMEN
2001

SYDNEY
1990

LA FEMME NIKITA
1997–2001; revival 2010–2013

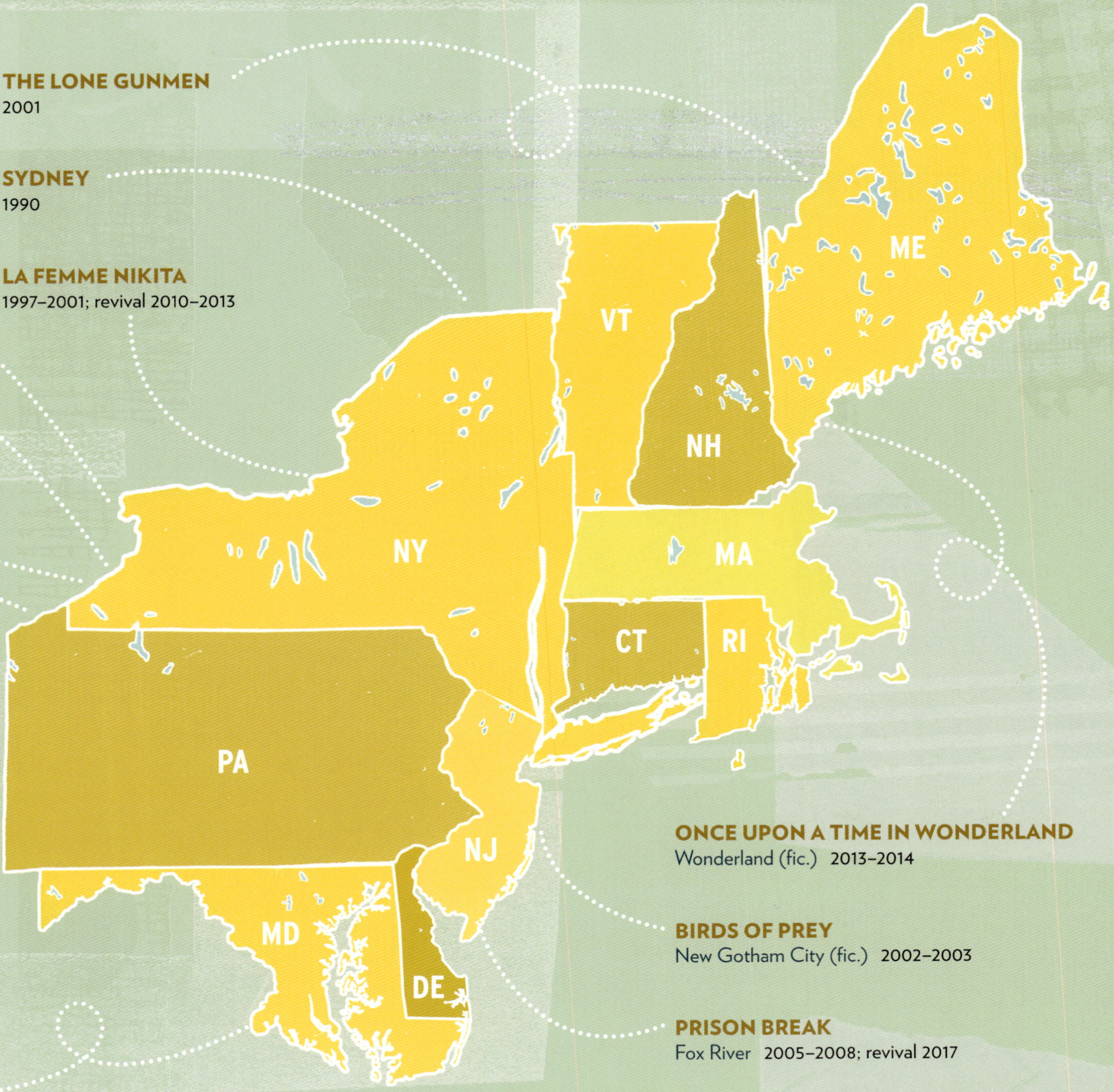

VT

ME

NH

NY

MA

CT

RI

PA

NJ

MD

DE

ONCE UPON A TIME IN WONDERLAND
Wonderland (fic.)   2013–2014

BIRDS OF PREY
New Gotham City (fic.)   2002–2003

PRISON BREAK
Fox River   2005–2008; revival 2017

THE CLEVELAND SHOW
Stoolbend   2009–2013

OK

TX

THE FLYING NUN
San Juan, PR   1967–1970
No trip to Puerto Rico is complete without a stop at the Santo Tanco convent, where you'll encounter nuns who are only too eager to help. Just be sure to hold on to your hats—it does tend to get very windy!

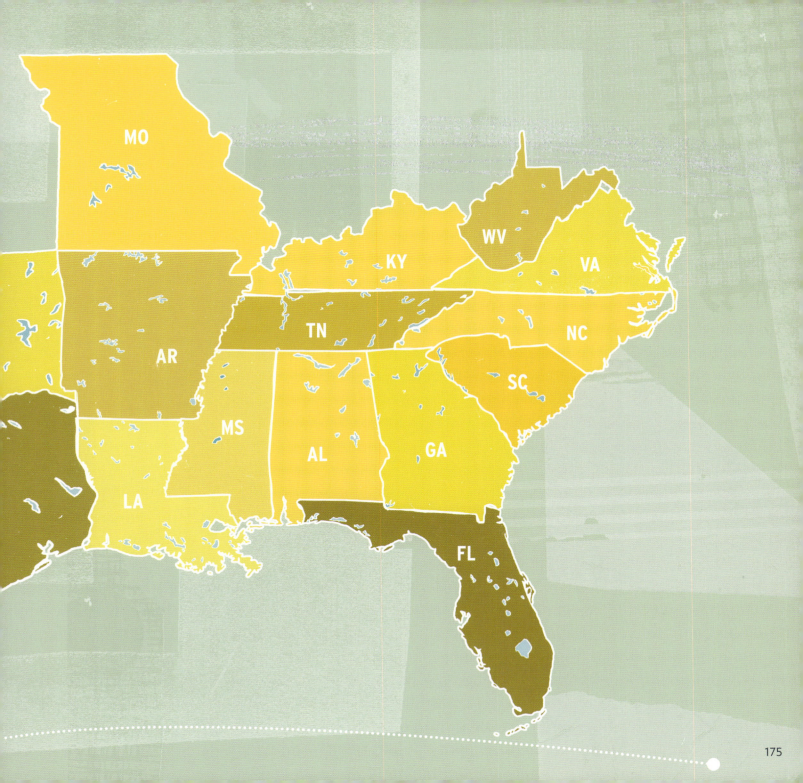

LOVE OF LIFE 1951–1980

GUIDING LIGHT Springfield (Fic) 1952–2009

FATHER KNOWS BEST Springfield 1954–1960

LASSIE Calverton (fic.) 1954–1973

HIGHWAY PATROL 1955–1959

THE EDGE OF NIGHT Monticello (fic.) 1956–1984

LEAVE IT TO BEAVER Mayfield (fic.) 1957–1963

THE FLINTSTONES Bedrock 1960–1966

BEN CASEY 1961–1966

DR. KILDARE 1961–1966

DAYS OF OUR LIVES Salem 1965–present

JULIA 1968–1971

BRIGHT PROMISE 1969–1972

SHAZAM! 1974–1976

THE HITCHHIKER 1983–1991

THE JETSONS
Orbit City (fic.) 1962–1963; revival 1985–1987

FINDER OF LOST LOVES
1984–1985

DOWN TO EARTH
1984–1987

21 JUMP STREET
Metropolis (fic.) 1987–1991

FRAGGLE ROCK
1983–1987

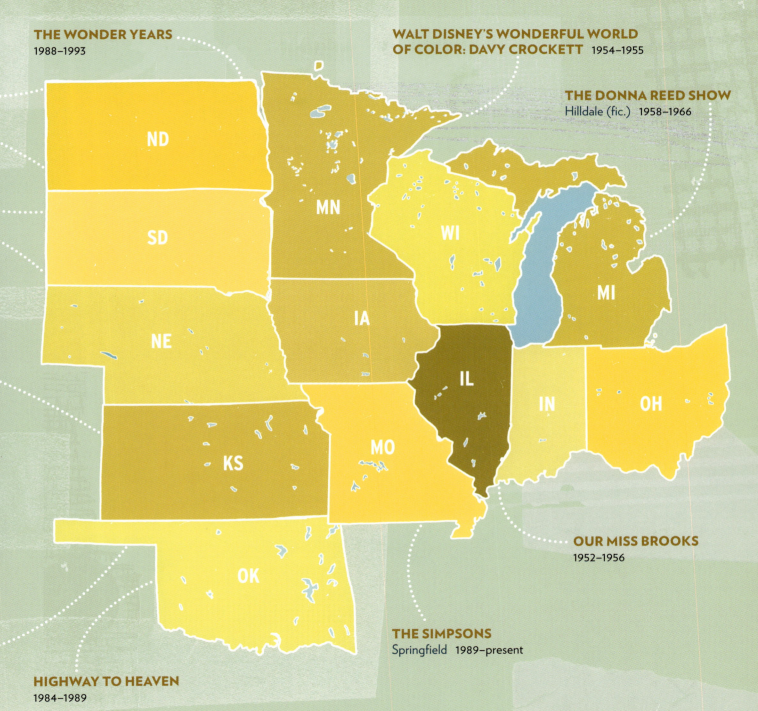

THE WONDER YEARS
1988–1993

WALT DISNEY'S WONDERFUL WORLD OF COLOR: DAVY CROCKETT   1954–1955

THE DONNA REED SHOW
Hilldale (fic.)   1958–1966

ND

SD

NE

KS

OK

MN

IA

MO

WI

MI

IL

IN

OH

OUR MISS BROOKS
1952–1956

THE SIMPSONS
Springfield   1989–present

HIGHWAY TO HEAVEN
1984–1989

THE MANY LOVES OF DOBIE GILLIS
Central City (fic.) 1959–1963

HIGHWAY PATROL
1955–1959

DILBERT 1999–2000

STRANGERS WITH CANDY
Flatpoint (fic.) 1999–2000

LIZZIE MCGUIRE 2001–2004

ALL GROWN UP 2003–2008

DANNY PHANTOM Amity Park (fic.) 2004–2007

MY NAME IS EARL Camden (fic.) 2005–2009

AARON STONE 2009–2010

BETTER OFF TED 2009–2010

RAISING HOPE Natesville (fic.) 2010–2014

CHILDRENS HOSPITAL 2010–2016

TERRA NOVA 2011

THE THUNDERMANS Hiddenville (fic.) 2013–2018

THE FLASH Central City (fic.) 2014–present

IF LOVING YOU IS WRONG 2014–present

GOOD WITCH Middleton (fic.) 2015–present

TALES FROM THE CRYPT
1989–1996

PARKER LEWIS CAN'T LOSE
1990–1993

CLARISSA EXPLAINS IT ALL
1991–1994

RUGRATS
1991–2004

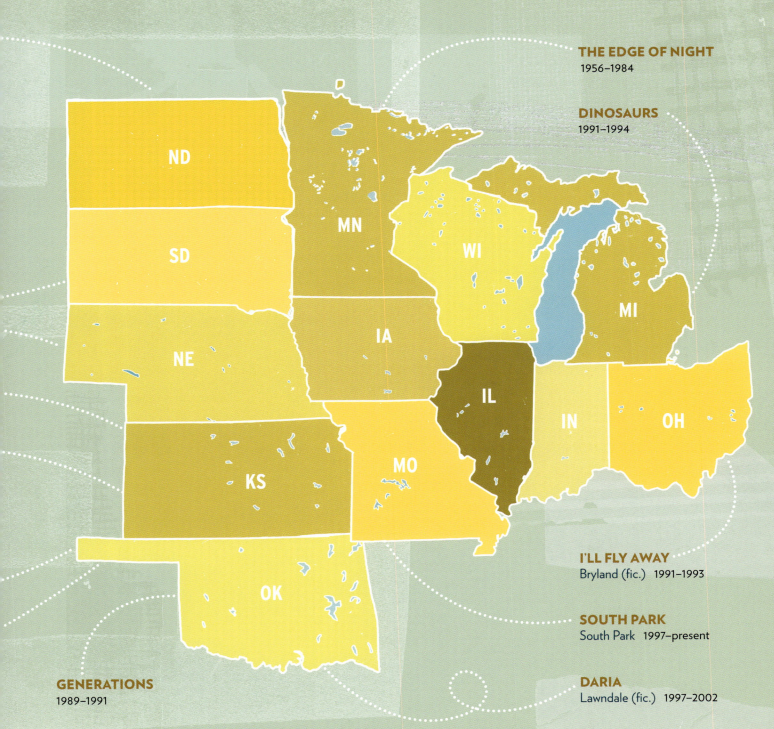

THE EDGE OF NIGHT
1956–1984

DINOSAURS
1991–1994

I'LL FLY AWAY
Bryland (fic.) 1991–1993

SOUTH PARK
South Park 1997–present

GENERATIONS
1989–1991

DARIA
Lawndale (fic.) 1997–2002

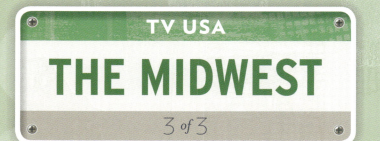
HIGH SCHOOL USA! 2013–2015

SUPERGIRL National City (fic.) 2015–present

CASUAL 2015–2018

CRIMINAL MINDS: BEYOND BORDERS
2016–2017

GOOD BEHAVIOR 2016–2017

BIZAARDVARK 2016–present

LEGENDS OF TOMORROW 2016–present

IMPOSTERS 2017–2018

LEGION 2017–present

13 REASONS WHY 2017–present

A SERIES OF UNFORTUNATE EVENTS
The City (fic.) 2017–present

ANDI MACK 2017–present

CHILLING ADVENTURES OF SABRINA
Greendale (fic.) 2018–present

BLACK LIGHTNING
Freeland 2018–present

THE MAN IN THE HIGH CASTLE
Canon City 2015–present

MALCOLM IN THE MIDDLE
2000–2006

RUGRATS: ALL GROWN UP
2003–2008

ROUTE 66
1960–1964

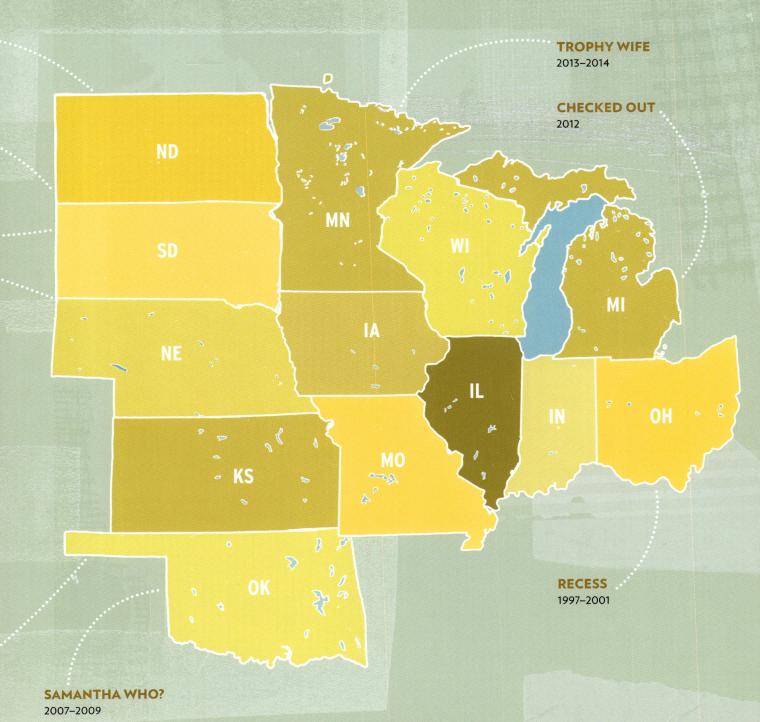

TROPHY WIFE
2013–2014

CHECKED OUT
2012

RECESS
1997–2001

SAMANTHA WHO?
2007–2009

AK

MAVERICK 1957–1962

F TROOP 1965–1967

THE WILD WILD WEST 1965–1969

KUNG FU 1972–1975

FANTASY ISLAND 1977–1984; revival 1998–1999

THE LOVE BOAT 1977–1986

9 TO 5 1982–1983; 1986–1988

TJ HOOKER 1982–1986

AIRWOLF 1984–1987

PEE-WEE'S PLAYHOUSE 1986–1990

BLOSSOM 1991–1995

ARLI$$ 1996–2002

PROFIT 1996

RAWHIDE
1959–1965

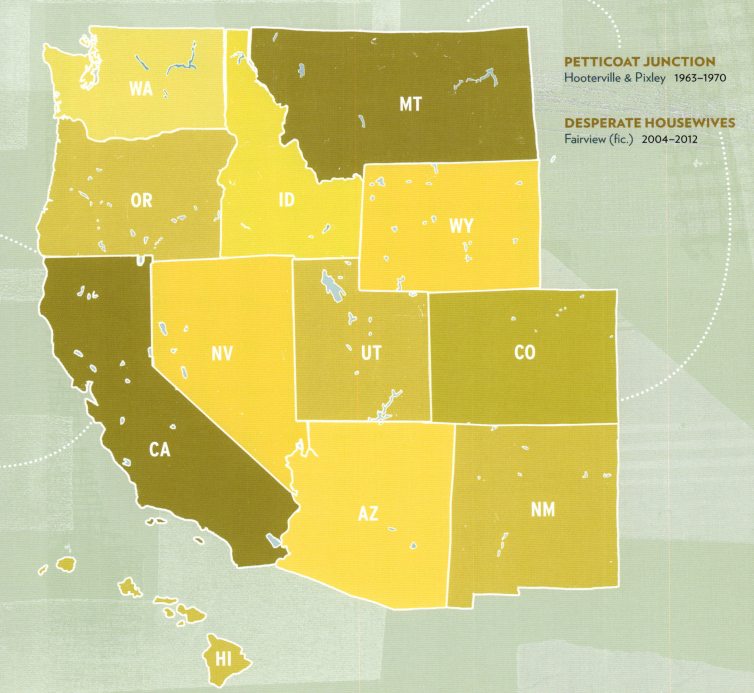

PETTICOAT JUNCTION
Hooterville & Pixley 1963–1970

DESPERATE HOUSEWIVES
Fairview (fic.) 2004–2012

WA

MT

OR

ID

WY

NV

UT

CO

CA

AZ

NM

HI

AK

MISSION: IMPOSSIBLE 1966–1973

THE PROUD FAMILY 2001–2005

SCRUBS 2001–2010

PHIL OF THE FUTURE 2004–2006

NED'S DECLASSIFIED SCHOOL SURVIVAL GUIDE 2004–2007

LOST 2004–2010

THE NEW ADVENTURES OF OLD CHRISTINE 2006–2010

CHARLIE'S ANGELS 2011

CONSTANTINE 2014–2015

BULL 2016–present

WESTWORLD 2016–present

WRECKED 2016–present

THE SIX MILLION DOLLAR MAN
1973–1978

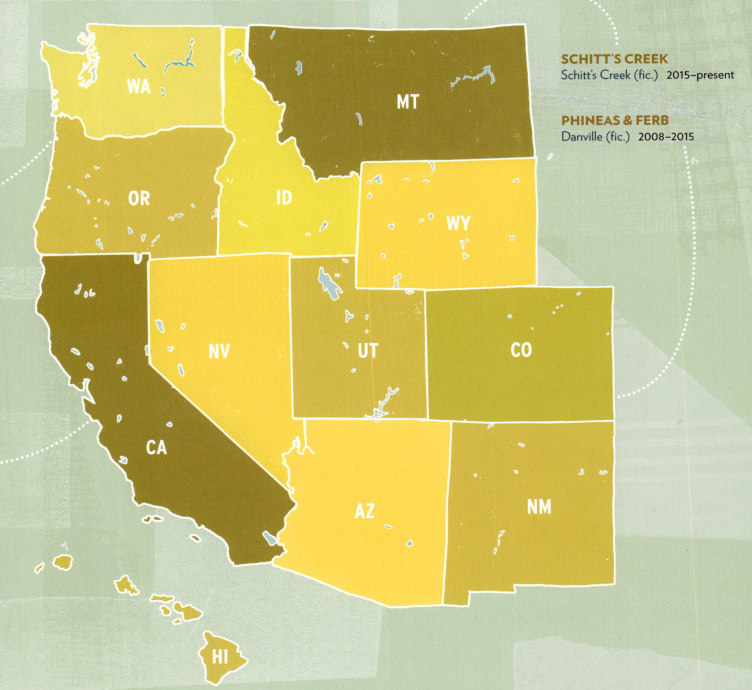

SCHITT'S CREEK
Schitt's Creek (fic.)   2015–present

PHINEAS & FERB
Danville (fic.)   2008–2015

WA

MT

OR

ID

WY

NV

UT

CO

CA

AZ

NM

HI

INDEX

THANKS AND ACKNOWLEDGMENTS

Road trips are always better with traveling companions, and this one was no exception. I'm grateful to John Deen, who set us on the road; and Katie Hands, Chip Carter, Colin Hough-Trapp, Jenn Thompson, Celina Carvalho, and Frank DeCaro for snacks, sing-alongs, and games of license plate bingo; and, of course, Kavel Rafferty, for providing the beautiful scenery. Thanks must be given to David and Oscar, who understand that watching television is part of my job, and my parents, who introduced me to laugh tracks, reruns, and that "See the U.S.A. in Your Chevorlet" song. Extra special thanks must be given to the best editorial and travel companion anyone could ever have, Jessica Fuller.

First published in the United States of America in 2019 by
Rizzoli International Publications, Inc.
300 Park Avenue South
New York, NY 10010
www.rizzoliusa.com

Photo on page 114 © and courtesy Magnolia Bakery
Photos on pages 20–21, 56–57, 80–81, 106–107, 146–146, 166–167 courtesy Getty Images
Design by Celina Carvalho

2019 2020 2021 2022 2023 / 10 9 8 7 6 5 4 3 2 1

Printed in China

ISBN-13: 978-0-7893-3653-8
Library of Congress Control Number: 2018963206